The I of the Storm

Also by Gary Simmons

Embrace Tiger—Return to Mountain:
Spiritual Conflict Management (audiocassette)

The **I** of the **Storm**

Embracing Conflict, Creating Peace

GARY SIMMONS

unity®
Books

Unity Village, MO 64065-0001

First edition 2001
Sixteenth printing 2011

To place an order, call the Customer Service Department: 1-800-236-3571 or go online at *www.unitybooks.org*.

The publisher wishes to acknowledge the editorial work of Michael Maday and Raymond Teague; the copy services of Thomas Lewin, Marlene Barry, and Mary Lou Kaltenbach; the production help of Rozanne Devine and Jane Turner; and the marketing efforts of Allen Liles, Dawn O'Malley, and Sharon Sartin.

Cover design by Cherie Peltier—Pimento Creative
Cover illustration by Rafael Lopez
Interior design by Coleridge Design

Library of Congress Control Number: 2001086907
ISBN 0-87159-270-3
ISBN 978-0-87159-270-5
Canada BN 13252 9033 RT

Dedication

To Nan, the life of my light

Acknowledgments

Any WORTHWHILE ENDEAVOR begins as an idea and ends with an outer accomplishment. Yet it's the *everywhere in between* where lives are changed and blessings garnered. I have been blessed by the writing of the book because it is a creation of Spirit. The spirits of friendship, love, encouragement, insight, awakening, discovery, discipline, and possibility are the influences behind, above, before, and between these pages.

I wish to thank first my former congregation, my friends at Unity of Fayetteville in Arkansas who so graciously released me to my ministry of reconciliation. Thank you, Peggy, Mark, Rose, Dave, Joseph, Kate, Kim, Carol, Annette, Theresa, David, Mary Alice, Charles, Harriet, Kathleen, Mike, John, Linda, Marilyn, Renée, Allie, Vic, Edith, J. C., Gennie, Beth, Raymond, and Sylvia.

Thanks also to my colleagues on the Association of Unity Churches Standards Committee, each of whom I owe a debt of gratitude for their willingness to believe in me. They were not only a source of encouragement and strength but helped make it possible that my work would have global impact. Thanks especially to Rev. Marilyn Muehlbach and Rev. Marleen Davis, who became my cheerleaders and soulmates as we envisioned a new paradigm for peacemaking in the Unity movement.

Then there are the champions themselves, the peace workers who have proved the principles of this book in their peacemaking. Thanks to Steve Towles, Claudell County, Nancy Worth, Mary Ann Finch, Max Lafser, John Butler III, Roger Goodwin, Diana Hughes, Audrey Bickford, Susan Gideonse, Victoria Lafser, Nancy Purcell, Robert Stocks, Kate Peppler, Ben Andrews, Juhlie Anderson, Patty Edwards, Margee Grounds, David and Alice Durksen, Donna Winchell, Lawrence Palmer, Kristine Broderhausen, Bonnie Gilbert-Ashe, Nellie Flemming, and Clare Austen.

Many others have touched me with their love, support, and encouragement as I have endeavored to journal the principles of conflict transformation. I wish to thank my boss, Dr. Glenn Mosley, president and CEO of the Association of Unity Churches, who has given me the freedom to create my passion. Thanks, too, to Rev. Carl Osier, M.D.; Rev. Joann Landreth; and the Association of Unity Churches staff for supporting me in every way. I am also indebted to church management consultant Barbara O'Hearne for her commitment to excellence.

Then there are my mentors, coaches, and friends, some who have gone the second mile with me when others might have given up. Thanks to Connie and Rod Welty for taking me in when I was homeless; to Doris Hoskins for being my buddy; to Beth Ann Suggs, who sat in the fire with me; to Maria Nemeth for gifting me with an awareness of my wholeness; to Thomas Crum for helping me truly see the magic in conflict. Thanks to Harry Payne and Grandmaster E. C. Ahn for teaching me about perseverance; to Dennis and Kit Neagle, who turned my world upside down; to my friends Craig and Barbara Oliver; and to Mardana Jones, who saw with me the best of times and the worst of times.

To my dear friend John Babbs, who has been my compass and pathfinder: Thank you, John, for your guidance, love, and insight. And to my colleague, brother, and coconspirator, Bill Williams: I thank you for turning my lights on.

Finally, I wish to thank my sweetie and wife, Nan; our kids; our families; my parents; and our furries. You are my greatest teachers and closest friends.

Table of Contents

Foreword

IMAGINE FOR A MOMENT a time before your birth when you were wandering the heavens as a disincarnate soul. You were immersed in the beauty and peaceful harmony of paradise when a call went out for volunteers to incarnate in bodily, human form. A small blue planet in the far reaches of the Milky Way galaxy was experiencing a crisis and was in need of souls who were willing to incarnate in a human body to help out in Earth's time of need.

You made the decision to volunteer. You next met with the Incarnation Committee to discuss with its members the part you wanted to play and the work you wanted to do. You made a covenant at that time to do the work you agreed to do. But there was a catch: Not only were you to serve, you were also required to *grow*. It was your job to increase the intensity of your light and to grow in wisdom and in stature as well as to serve. You next had to make a series of decisions that would perfectly situate you to be of maximum service and to develop a custom-designed learning curriculum for your soul to assure its maximum learning potential.

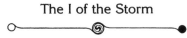

You had to decide what particular set of gifts, talents, and abilities you wished to bring with you to contribute to life on Earth and to the human family; the dreams and aspirations that would lead you to your destiny to fulfill your earthly covenant; a date of birth determining an astrological configuration that would give you clues to your soul's earthly purpose and destiny; a place on Earth, a climatic zone, a region in which to reside; a racial and ethnic form that would enable you to best express yourself; a socioeconomic class that would provide you with the challenges and benefits you need in order to learn and serve; a spiritual tradition with its particular set of rituals and practices that would support you; a gender with its attendant opportunities and challenges; a particular set of parents that would provide you with their particular strengths, with qualities that you could draw upon and with a designed set of difficulties that you would experience with them in order to learn, grow, and to prepare you for the service that you are to perform; your siblings and your relationship to them in age, plus the companionship and the conflicts with them that would provide you with important lessons and resources; and, finally, a name for yourself.

Once these decisions were made, you were free to incarnate and begin your earthly mis-

sion, forgetting all that went on before, but with time, you would slowly but surely begin to re-discover why you are here and how wisely you chose because *every* factor in your life has per-fectly positioned you for the service you are to perform and has maximized your potential for learning and growing.

This guided imagery, first developed by Dr. Carol Woman, I often use with the execu-tives and professionals whom I mentor and counsel. I find that so many of my clients come to a juncture in their lives when they begin to think, as the ancient, mystical Sufi poet Rumi stated almost eight hundred years ago, "Where did I come from, and what am I supposed to be doing?" In contemporary terms, the people with whom I work often come to a place in their lives where, despite all of their accomplish-ments and achievements, they begin to ques-tion the meaning and purpose of their lives. This is where I often am extended an invitation to their lives. Often, I tell them this tale and ask them to begin to reflect upon their lives. It is at this point where they begin to assemble the an-swers to their questions about the meaning and purpose of their lives.

This is where Gary Simmons' book *The I of the Storm* becomes so valuable and essential. For it is not just with the answering of these questions of meaning and purpose alone that

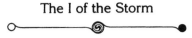
a person becomes content. In some respects the challenges in a person's life become even greater. If one has a clear sense of purpose and direction for his or her life, that life must still be lived and enacted within the dynamics of the human condition—with all its attendant pressures, contradictions, and conflicts. When one was asleep or only dimly aware of his or her purpose and direction, these conflicts and paradoxes were not as apparent as they become with a greater understanding of one's purpose and personal destiny.

I love the way that Gary weaves in his experience in the martial arts with his clear understanding of spiritual principles. It often *does* seem that the path we are asked to walk in this life is the path of the spiritual warrior. We are always being asked to remember our divine nature and our spiritual commitment, as simultaneously we are asked to face the challenges that life presents us. Life often screams at us: "Do it my way!" The path of spiritual warriors is to calmly and peacefully, while looking into the mouth of the dragon, remember who we really are—divine emissaries—and to think, feel, and act accordingly.

The Sufis say that the two rivers of Heaven and Earth converge in the human heart. The heart is the bridge between Heaven and Earth.

But in the midst of this turbulence, where these two rivers converge, we are asked to remain clear and centered and to become the spiritual warriors that we are all asked to be, remembering who we are and—in that moment, in the attendant confusion and disorder that appear before us—being the channels of light, love, and healing power that we are meant to be. God is love and we are God's emissaries sent to Earth to be the vehicles through which this light, love, and healing power can be expressed.

It is one thing to know this, quite another to live it. This is the magic of *The I of the Storm*. Gary, in a very practical, day-to-day, reality-based manner, discusses the challenges, temptations, and hazards the world presents to us that distract us from our purpose. Gary is able to give us, through his book, very practical techniques, both spiritually and materially based, for remembering who we are and what our mission on Earth is. He also takes us through the next step by giving us very practical strategies on how to avoid these hazards and how to align ourselves with our divine purpose and mission.

Finding this place and actuating it is essential to our beings. It not only gives a meaning and purpose to our lives but also allows us to grow, as Jesus did, in wisdom and stature and in favor with God and with humanity. It also al-

lows us to increase the intensity of the illumi-
nation of the light we brought with us when we
came into this earthly existence.

If we are able to fully become the Knights
of Light and Love that we are meant to be, we
will leave life on Earth and the human family a
little better for our having walked this journey
for a brief moment during the expanse of eter-
nity. Life will be better for our having been here.
Life will inch a little closer to the divine ideal of
love, harmony, and beauty because of our walk.

John Babbs
March 2000

John Babbs advises business executives and provides
organizational-development and strategic-planning services to midsized organizations. He also is the author
of *The Divine Hotline.*

Introduction

No ONE IS AGAINST YOU. This is the absolute Truth. You may not believe it now. You may have a lifetime of evidence to the contrary. But until you realize that the entire universe is *for* you, you may never experience your wholeness and true worth. The purpose of this book is to awaken you to the Truth that there is only one presence and power at work in your life, and that this presence and power lives in you as the Spirit of God. For this reason no one or nothing can be against you. To realize this is to claim your divine inheritance as a beloved creation of God.

How This Book Will Help You

Self-help books usually contain exercises and how-tos as a means of effecting healing and personal transformation. In the arena of creating harmony and living from wholeness, I will share two useful methods of integrating the principles of this book.

The first method is what I call "aware-therapy," or *aware-apy*. At the end of each chapter are questions or exercises that will help you examine your thought processes and belief system. An example of an aware-apy question is, "How is it possible to be afraid?" As you attempt to answer this question, you will first recall situations that have felt threatening. You may then look deeper and notice that present fears are rooted in past issues. As you continue to explore the question, you may discover that fear is only possible when you don't feel connected to your sense of wholeness and worth, or when you don't see God in the situation. Your effort to be with the question is a kind of aware-therapy and helps you break up the solidified metaphors that reinforce your belief system. If you can see that fear is not so much evidence of danger, but rather an indication you are not connected to God, you may respond differently to a threat the next time one arises. Unless someone has a gun to your head

or a knife to your throat, defensiveness rooted in fear only reinforces your sense of separation.

The second method is working with the principle of *center*. Centering helps you to embrace difficult situations without becoming defensive or reactive. Centering is a body/mind dynamic. Your body must be relaxed and your mind must be capable of shifting attention and awareness in order not to create resistance. The shifting of attention and awareness is key to moving from center. If you look into a car window on a bright and sunny day, you easily see your reflection. With a little effort, you can shift your attention to become aware of what is inside the vehicle. We are conditioned to see the reflection first, because how we "look" or how we are being perceived is what matters most to us. Seeing beyond the reflection and into the interior of an issue requires a willingness to look harder and in a new way. This is what I mean by shifting attention and awareness to center. From center, we see, say, and do something entirely different from what we see, say, and do when relating to the reflection.

CHAPTER ONE

No One Is Against You

MANY YEARS AGO I WAS INVITED to host a public lecture featuring two Hindu ascetics of the Maharishi Jyotish order who were brought to the United States by two Arkansas residents in the process of establishing an Ayurvedic university. As a minister and as a student of Eastern philosophy and religion, I was happy to accommodate the request and welcomed my distinguished guests with enthusiasm and reverence.

The following week I received a phone call from one of the university organizers, asking if I would be interested in meeting privately with the Jyotish, who wished to give me a complimentary consultation in appreciation for my hospitality. The Jyotish is an ancient order of Hindu astrologers. According to legend, the

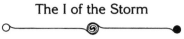

Jyotish lineage is over five thousand years old. Jyotish astrology uses a unique cosmology that accepts the presence of two invisible celestial bodies in addition to the planets of Western astrology. These invisible planets are believed to exert powerful influences upon all sentient beings.

I agreed to the meeting, in part out of respect and also out of curiosity, to see if the ascetics could actually tell me something about myself. We met in a small office that smelled of incense and was decorated with traditional Hindu art. The sounds of sitar music softly played in the background. Through an interpreter, Muhru and Satchi explained that the purpose of our meeting was not to *forecast* my future, but to *awaken* my future. To do this, they would first need to demonstrate that their science was profoundly accurate. They asked me to think of five significant events, five passions, and five disappointments in my life and to write them down. They waited in silence as I completed my list. For the next hour Muhru and Satchi recounted my past, in vivid detail and with chilling accuracy. To my amazement, they touched upon every item on my list. How was it possible, I thought to myself, they could determine from reading my birthchart that I was building an airplane, that I was a martial artist, and that I had had several failed marriages?

I suddenly felt embarrassed, vulnerable, and uncomfortable as they continued. Muhru turned to face me. His compassion and softness melted my resistance and I relaxed. "No one is against you," he said, "not even your own life." I didn't understand what he was saying, at first. Was Muhru attributing my uneasiness to how I was feeling about myself? I asked the translator to explain that I was awestruck by their accuracy and a little nervous at the prospect that my future could be so easily discerned. Next, Satchi spoke, assuring me that no one's future is etched in stone. The future can only be regarded as probabilities floating upon a sea of infinite possibilities.

"What makes us so predictable," he added, "is that attention and awareness continuously reframe the present moment in the context of past influences. Who we are today is what sets tomorrow's stage. Consciousness is poured into the creative framework of attention and awareness to set into motion the forces that organize the manifest universe. If consciousness is in bondage to the past or if attention is mesmerized according to ingrained patterns of awareness, the future is simply an extended line from here into tomorrow—and that's what makes the future predictable."

Muhru and Satchi then offered to answer any questions I might have. I asked them to tell me what I needed to know about my future so

I could begin *then* to walk my spiritual path more authentically. They smiled as the translator relayed my request. To my surprise, Muhru began to speak in English, "What have your past wife experiences taught you?" Past *wife* experiences? Surely he meant past *life* experiences. I didn't remember any past life experiences. "No, not past life, *past wife* experiences," Muhru returned. I laugh now at the expression *past wife experience.* I guess I have learned that I can't look outside myself for wholeness and completion. Each *wife* experience has given me insight into how I have placed the burden of my well-being on someone else.

Muhru continued: "Can you see how everything that is *for* you or *against* you has its roots within you? As you have learned, your wholeness can't be found outside of you. Are you also willing to see that lack and abundance are not outside of you either? Can you see that your struggle for wholeness and worth has been predicated upon the belief that there are opposing forces at work in your life? Do people—your wife, your children, your parents, colleagues, friends, or even strangers on the street—hold a measure of your well-being hostage? And in your attempts to find yourself, to get what you need, or to feel safe and okay, must you first gain the cooperation, approval, or acceptance of others?"

Satchi spoke through the translator: "No one is against you. You have no adversary in your life. There is nothing in the universe that is against you or your purpose. This is what is meant by an 'awakened' future. You must leave this room knowing only one thing—that nothing is against you. Nothing opposes you. Any experience you may have to the contrary is evidence that your mind is rooted in separation and illusion. If you resist what seems to resist you, you strengthen the hypnotism that keeps you in bondage to your past and makes predictable your future."

Muhru added in English: "No one is against you. Make your path be about proving this truth, and you will discover what wholeness really is."

How Can This Be True?

How can this be true, considering all the challenges and problems we face in our lives? I thought to myself. Is not our world filled with adversaries—people or situations that resist us, threaten us, or take advantage of us? In a world where lovers quarrel, parents argue, children fight, families feud, students protest, and nations war, how can it be true that no one is against us?

In my thirty years of practicing martial arts,

I have broken my fingers, wrists, ankles, toes, and ribs. I have been knocked out, choked unconscious, stabbed, and cut open—all in the *practice* of martial arts. I have never been actually attacked by someone trying to hurt me!

In my relationships with others, I have had my heart broken, my butt kicked, my ego bruised. I've been stabbed in the back by a friend, raked over the coals by a boss, and pounced upon by my wife. I've been crushed, stepped on, left hanging, and blasted. Isn't it interesting that the metaphors we use to describe our relationship difficulties seem to assume that we really *are* being attacked? Our lives are filled with real and imagined dangers, or so it seems. Is it any wonder that we have created a *virtual* reality out of our fears and insecurities and superimposed it upon the landscape of our daily lives?

Is your field of dreams mined, booby-trapped, or filled with hostile forces waiting to ambush you? Do you dread venturing out into the sea of infinite possibilities, afraid of being torpedoed and sunk midway in your voyage toward fulfillment? Indeed, it is understandable how we tend to armor ourselves when life looks and feels scary.

When someone threatens you and you feel defensive, do you use your own feelings of fear

and defensiveness as evidence that the person must really be against you? If someone blames you or accuses you, do you react to protect yourself? All of us (to some degree) do this, because our human nature is governed by the need to be safe and feel okay. But is the person who threatens you or judges you or discounts you *really* against you? And is your defensive posture the best way to manage these uncomfortable moments? Is it possible that the experience of intimidation, threat, or adversarial relationships arises out of *how you are relating to the experience*, and *not how the experience is relating to you?*

Searching for What's Missing

It's not easy to see this directly. We think of ourselves as innocent bystanders, minding our own business, when suddenly we find ourselves victims of circumstances. The stance of defensiveness is justified, given the nature of the environment in which we live.

Yet we know our insecurities and self-protection strategies are rooted in a deep sense of incompleteness. If we were whole (we imagine), if we had confidence and personal power, the seeming hostilities of our world could be managed—if not conquered. And so we attribute our weaknesses and vulnerabilities to the apparent missing pieces in our sense of wholeness and worth. Not knowing specifically what to search for, we find that our quests for what's missing center upon issues of well-being. What do I need in order to feel safe and okay? is the question that guides our search for completion.

Searching for wholeness in terms of what's missing or what completes you creates a hypersensitivity to how life looks and feels. You are driven to avoid what makes you feel unsafe and compelled to hold on to what seemingly completes you. In this paradigm, you are only whole when you feel good about yourself, when you are successful, when you have enough money, or when you are happy. But, is this really wholeness? Is wholeness something that can be here today and gone tomorrow?

A W A R E - A P Y

1. Take a few minutes to consider the title of this chapter, "No One Is Against You." What thoughts and feelings arise? How has your life seemed against you at times? What are the common themes?
2. How comfortable are you with conflict? What kinds of situations put you on the defensive?
3. Make a list of inner resources. What inner resource do you need in order to manage threatening situations better? Is it confidence or worthiness or self-acceptance?
4. Look at your list of inner resources. They are attributes of your wholeness and worth. Think of times in your past when you felt connected to these resources. For instance, think about the last time you felt confident. What were the circumstances? Now imagine a situation when you felt threatened. Pretend that in this situation you were confident, instead of fearful or defensive. Imagine how you might relate to the situation or person differently if you felt connected to this inner resource.
5. How much energy do you spend protecting or defending yourself? How safe and okay do you feel? Imagine that your energy is like gas in your car's

tank. At the end of the day, how full or empty is your tank?

6. Make a list of some of the funny or not-so-funny things you have done to avoid conflict.

7. Imagine that you are a sage. What advice would you give to someone who asks, "How do I avoid or prevent conflict?"

CHAPTER TWO

The I of the Storm

A New Paradigm for Wholeness

IN A SPIRITUAL CONTEXT, wholeness is the energy of communion, principle, purpose, and nonresistance—ideas that I will expand upon later. Wholeness is not outside of you, nor is it separate from you. It is the essence of your true nature and spiritual identity. And because wholeness is the foundation of your being, nothing can oppose you.

I will help you see that what arises as an adversary in your life comes from within you. Seeing this is not a bad thing. It's important you know *how* you are creating resistance and tension in your life. It's important to see the rela-

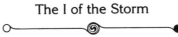

tionship between thoughts of fear and lack and how they manifest themselves as experiences, appearing as if someone or something is against you. And it's necessary to take responsibility for your fear-based actions and the hurt they may have caused. You cannot experience your wholeness believing that someone or something is against you. You cannot experience inner peace when you are worried that something isn't right with your world. As students of Truth, we must eventually reconcile ourselves to the principle that there is no force in the universe which opposes the life each of us is meant to live.

While the world is truly a place of opposites and competing tensions, these forces are not a power over us. Conflicts, challenges, and interpersonal difficulties are dynamic energies within which we can move authentically and appropriately, so long as we remember that these forces aren't against us.

The I of the Storm

Conflict and interpersonal difficulty are like a storm system that arises when two weather fronts converge. There is displacement, movement, and friction. The forces within the system build in intensity as temperature, dew point, wind velocity, barometric pressure, jet stream,

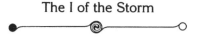

humidity, and landscape combine to form a distinct rotation of influence. A hurricane is born. Similarly, competing needs, wants, and values—combined with misperception, defensiveness, and the need to be right—create an energetic field of influence that is the storm inherent in interpersonal conflict.

At the center of the hurricane is its eye—a single theoretical point in space where the forces of the storm are in perfect equilibrium. At the eye, there is peace, calm, clarity, and stillness. The storm of conflict also possesses a center. I call this center the *I of the Storm.* As you can surmise from this analogy, the *I* of the storm is your wholeness and spiritual essence. It is where you can experience the storm without resisting it. At the circumference of the storm, the winds of confusion, blame, and the need to be right blow with devastating ferocity. The center, the *I* of the storm, is where you experience peace, clarity, stillness, and calm. If there is a storm in your life, you can know that you and your wholeness are at the center of it. Knowing this, you can stop resisting or making wrong those who seem to be against you. You can, instead, shift your attention and awareness, and you can experience the conflict from the center, where you are capable of authentic and principled action.

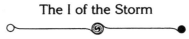

Lest We Forget

In the course of presenting workshops and conflict-transformation training to audiences throughout the world, I have witnessed first-hand the difficulty people have in applying spiritual principles to interpersonal conflicts. Disputants within conflicted church communities will commonly blame one another for not "walking their talk." In one such community the membership was engaged in an angry debate over how funds from a bequest would be spent. Tempers flared as members accused one another of hidden agendas. Some threatened to leave the church, while others hinted of legal action. During the course of the meeting, a teenager asked to speak to her church family. "If we can't make peace in a Unity church," she began, "if we can't practice our teaching here in our spiritual home, what hope is there for the world?" It took a child to wake up the church. It took a child to help them remember their purpose and why they were a church in the first place.

The same is true for you and me. We must remember that we are spiritual beings having a human experience. Nothing is against us. When we find ourselves in conflict, we need to examine how it is possible that we have created an adversary, when the entire universe conspires to fulfill itself through us.

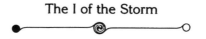

Twenty-five years ago I attended a workshop in which the lecturer stated, "Life is all about mind over matter—if you don't mind, it don't matter!" We all laughed. Later, I began to ponder this statement and mused at its implication. We have a choice in how we interpret our life experiences. Perhaps this is our major contribution to the quality of our lives. Our explanations, assumptions, and judgments mediate how we relate to any given situation. This poignant observation led me to the following realization: I *make my life mean what it means.* The way *I* choose to relate to my experience is what *my* experience becomes. The quality of my life, its inherent ambiance, arises from within me.

What I See Is What I Get

In ordinary terms, life appears to happen to us. We do not see ourselves as distinct from our experiences. Why is this so? It is because the mechanics of perception and awareness create this relationship. As observers, we find ourselves the object of events and circumstances. Things happen. *We* react. Yet, underlying the apparent domino effect of daily life, we are thinking and feeling. Our thoughts and feelings create mental and emotional states that influence how we relate or respond to what is happening. We project onto events and circumstances mean-

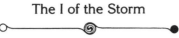

ing and relevance. Someone cuts in front of us in traffic. We get annoyed. We believe our annoyance comes from the inconsiderate driver. His recklessness is causing our reaction. But a deeper look into how our minds work reveals that the emotional response—annoyance— arises from what we make the situation mean. Would we have the same response if we knew, for instance, that the driver was speeding to take his pregnant wife to the hospital?

This invisible realm of meaning and relevance is what we bring to each event horizon. It may seem that we are innocent bystanders and that life happens to us, but it only appears this way.

Life happens *through us*. What *we* make of any situation makes it seem as if the situation exists independently of our influence. I once saw a T-shirt quoting Albert Einstein: "Only those who can see the invisible can do the impossible." Seeing the invisible, therefore, means seeing the relationship between one's *viewing point* and the factors that create a person's life experience. Our viewing point is like a rearview mirror captioned with the words "Objects are closer than they appear." It obscures how things really are, and we have become used to this distortion. The simple act of noticing something brings our attention into acute focus. And because our frame

of reference is always ourselves, we are at the center of our attention.

Experience is personalized because we make it about us. This is no small matter when we consider that how we relate to our life experiences is what drives our behavior. What I do, why I do it, and what my life becomes have roots in what I *believe* is happening to me. It is this invisible, causal realm of consciousness that is the energy of belief we must learn to see and recognize as influencing our life experiences. Beliefs mediate our attention and awareness, and therefore determine our viewing point. *Not seeing* the invisible at work in our lives and not understanding that the meanings we attribute to what is perceived affect our life experiences keep us from shifting our attention to new and healthier viewing points. This form of "blindness" creates a reactive orientation to life and diminishes our willingness to embrace life on its own terms.

Gaps in Awareness

Because all human perception is incomplete, how you see things involves a process of filling in the *gaps* in your awareness. You don't always know what's going on or what's happening. You compensate by filling in the missing pieces in your awareness with your own beliefs, thoughts, and impressions. You can't see what's motivating the harried driver, so you assume he is an inconsiderate jerk. Why do you fill in the gaps with negative assumptions? When the phone rings at 3 A.M., why do you fear the worst instead of being hopeful? When there are gaps to be filled, your mind naturally accesses the information it has. It reaches into beliefs, memory, and deep impressions. It scans the database of your mind for a possible correlation between what the situation is and what it might mean to you. It brings to the surface of your awareness any number of assumptions that can be used as a basis of relating to the moment. If no correlation is forthcoming, your imagination will kick in. You will make the situation mean something that is relative to your own sense of well-being and worth.

Your mind compensates for these gaps by asking questions and making assumptions based upon your past experiences and how you feel about yourself: What's going on with this driver? Doesn't he know how unsafe he is? You may recall a terrible wreck or feel your heart pound as you brake to adjust to his maneuver. The meaning becomes real and your well-being becomes a central issue, because the gaps in your awareness compel you to make up the difference. As demonstrated in this next story, when

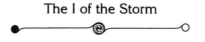

you fill in the gaps with your worst fears, you run the risk of creating your worst nightmares.

A minister of a large church became suspicious of his board president's intentions after learning that she had called a special meeting during the minister's absence. Rev. Tom's suspicion became more concrete when the board president cancelled a routine luncheon with no prior notice or explanation. Later, the minister discovered that she had been snooping around in his office after hours. The church secretary confided that the board president seemed secretive and overly concerned at being discovered. The minister imagined that the board was conspiring against him. He began to piece together other events and conversations that supported the possibility of hidden agendas. He felt certain that his job was in jeopardy and that the board would demand his resignation.

At the end of the week he received a call from the treasurer informing him of a special meeting of the board to be held immediately following Sunday services. He asked the treasurer about the meeting and was told the meeting would be brief and to the point.

Tom found little comfort in the applause from his congregation following his sermon entitled "Believing in Yourself." While the congregants were going through the receiving line, he was preoccupied with what would become of the church and his congregation. He wouldn't leave without a fight, he thought to himself.

Tom entered the boardroom and, unlike Daniel in the den of lions, he was nervous and afraid of confronting his adversaries. Sally, the board president, asked Tom to open the meeting with prayer. His hands were cold. He felt embarrassed as all joined hands in a circle for prayer. Sally began by apologizing to Tom for the board's not being more open and forthright in its deliberations, but she said that, given the circumstances before it, the board had decided to conduct its business in executive session.

Sally continued with recognizing Tom's accomplishments, the ways he had been a blessing to so many, and the extent to which he would be missed should circumstances arise that would cause him to leave the church. Tom braced himself as he listened. Sally looked at her fellow board members as she announced to Tom the board's unanimous decision to recommend to the membership that the church purchase a luxury home for their minister in appreciation for his many years of dedicated service to the church. In addition, the home would be gifted to the minister. Tom sank, speechless, into his chair. Tears filled his eyes. His only consolation in the midst of overwhelming embarrassment was that he had not given in to the urge to rally supporters in a campaign of ousting his mutinous board.

Have you ever had an experience like Tom's? It's easy to project onto your family and friends your own insecurities and fears. The inner workings of attention and awareness are the structure of a pseudo "virtual reality." However, if you are to live from your wholeness, you must first learn to see—to *see* how you are looking at your life. Then you must free yourself of having to interact with the images that arise from your conditioned mind.

To See or Not to See

What keeps you from being fully present to life, and therefore fully alive, is what's hidden in *you*, not in life. Life is abundant. It is only in your sense of separation that you feel threatened, limited, or fragmented. When you realize this, it is crucial to observe the dualistic thoughts and feelings that define your viewing point in terms of beliefs in good and evil. As you notice how your mind looks at life, you determine which beliefs are giving you a false impression. If your reactions or your meanings are rooted in how you see yourself *in relationship to your experience,* you can transform your experience by *choosing* to see the situation differently. This is an important tool—choice. In each moment of awareness, you choose how to direct your attention. You can choose to look differently at your experience and reframe what you

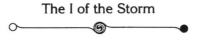

see. Like looking at a car window, you have to choose to look differently to see through the reflection. You can see the situation right before trying to make it right, because what is "wrong" with any given situation may very well be rooted in how you are relating to the experience, and not in the experience itself. Examine your meanings and decide if they are in alignment with the Truth. This process of self-examination and decision is a key principle in becoming present to life and finding your center, a principle that will be explored in detail later.

A House Divided Against Itself

Whatever supports your ability to be present to life, to embrace, serves all of humanity. This is no small endeavor, and it is for this reason that you must ask yourself if you have difficulty showing up to life. Do you avoid meeting life face-to-face? Have you become hardened to life and to others, resistant to change, or skillful at avoiding conflict? What supports your defensiveness, negativity, insecurity, and codependence?

One response that can shed light on these issues involves your struggle to integrate your spirituality with your human nature. You are a "house divided against itself" when you are caught between what moves you into action and what freezes you in the moment. Humanly,

you are motivated to get your needs met, to feel safe and okay about yourself. Spiritually, you are moved by a transcendent purpose that is selfless and thereby motivated from on high. Your soul's intention is to connect, embrace, and serve the Divine, regardless of how scary it feels. These two intentions—the drive to get your needs met and the impulse to connect, embrace, and serve—often compete. The tension created by these two forces brings you to the *edge* of your resourcefulness in moments of challenge or change. When you perceive a threat, your soul pushes you to confront your fears because fear keeps you small and reinforces your sense of separation. If you succeed in circumventing a dreaded encounter, you may have accomplished your goal to feel safe at the expense of cementing your suspicion into fact. If you feel insecure in a relationship, you may attempt to control your partner's actions. If you succeed, not only do you strain the relationship, you also reinforce that part of you which feels threatened by your partner's freedom.

You Have Experiences; Experiences Don't Have You

Your soul moves you toward challenges because they stretch you in ways that separate you from your falsehoods and dependencies. What you discover is that *you are not your ex-*

periences. You are greater. This distinction—
I am not my experience—is a key principle in
discovering your wholeness.

Often we use our condition or situation as
evidence of our well-being and worth. I become
less or more because of what happens to me. If
I lose my job, get sick, or fail in a relationship,
I may confuse these events with myself. I may
become depressed or defeated. Yet, in Truth, I
am not my experience. I may be challenged by
what happens in my life, but I am always
greater than my challenges. My circumstances
may appear limiting or difficult, but I am not
bound by external conditions, because I am
Spirit. In Spirit, conditions are mental structures.
In Spirit, limitations are fragmented possibilities. Nothing is an obstacle to Spirit because
conditions arise as an activity of Spirit seeking
to catch our attention so we may discover our
true lives in God.

Experiences are metaphors and mirrors of
your belief system, and they serve as feedback
to what you are making your life mean. They
are portals, breaking and breakthrough points
intended to awaken you to your own magnifi-
cence. They are not solid, but appear to be so
when they are resisted. They have no power in
and of themselves, but become powerful when
you fear them or make them seem to be against
you.

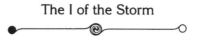

The Challenge to Become Present

Transforming the challenges in our lives requires of us the ability to become present to life with greater courage and strength. The movement toward becoming one global community has brought humanity to the edge of its resourcefulness. An interplanetary visitor might find our world an enigma. How is it possible that so many in the human family are suffering, while there is comfort enough to soothe the afflicted? How is it possible that there is so little food and safe drinking water for nearly two-thirds of the world, when the Earth shares so freely of its abundance? How is it possible that our inhumanity to each other is tolerated and frequently defended?

The growing disparity between the haves and the have-nots is creating global tension. All of us are touched by terrorism, ethnic violence, racism, unstable governments, and failing economies. Tension begets defensiveness. Defensiveness begets divisiveness. Yet the growing polarization within society is symptomatic. It is evidence of humanity undergoing transition and rebirth. Conflict and adversity are our midwives. Our painful labor becomes ever more excruciating as we struggle to reconcile our human frailties and character defects with our innate wholeness. This reconciliation—the integration

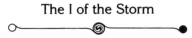

of our spirituality with our human condition—
is the remedy for a troubled world, for if it is
materially possible to ease suffering, feed the
hungry, shelter the afflicted, and protect the
vulnerable but we are not doing it, it may be
because we have yet to think of ourselves as
whole beings. We have yet to discover the tre-
mendous, awesome power of the presence of
God at our center, at the core of every life experience. It is this integration of Spirit and humanity that constitutes infinite and eternal life.
Jesus spoke of having life "abundantly," but a
truly abundant life is only possible in the un-
bridled passion of Spirit expressing Itself in the
midst of the seeming impossible. In the face of
adversity, where humanity meets the impossible, Spirit beckons us to come alive, to show
up to life, to become present.

Living From Lack

In the Gospel of Thomas it is written: "If
you bring forth what is within you, what you
have will save you. If you do not have that
within you, what you do not have within you
will kill you" (Thom. 70:1–2). Nearly every ill
we face in our daily lives and in our human
family can be linked to a belief in lack. In a very
real sense, *what we do not have* may be killing
us. We worry about paying our bills, about our

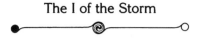

security in the future. We hurry because we believe there is not enough time. We burn out for lack of energy. We get passed by because we think we are not smart enough or good-looking enough. We fail because we believe we don't have what it takes. At every turn, our well-being is held hostage or liberated by what we make our experiences mean. And so, we become driven to compensate for what we lack or what seems to be our incompleteness. It is this driven lifestyle that is wearing us out.

Living in the illusion of lack also compels us to avoid conflict. When we don't feel okay about ourselves, when we feel inferior, when deep down inside we feel flawed, we are actually spiritually impoverished. We move away from challenges, instead of embracing them. It is this sense of lack, of not having, that destroys us. This inadequacy directs our attention outward and draws us to an addictive, codependent, and driven lifestyle. There is never enough time, energy, money, resources, or creativity in the presence of the black hole of inner being. When we, at the core of our being, feel we are not enough, nothing outside of us can complete or fulfill us. It is this missing sense of spiritual Self, the wholeness we seek, that we must come to know as our most valuable possession. We must become like the merchant who, finding the pearl of great price, gladly sells all she

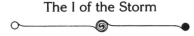
has to acquire it. More than anything that can be possessed, our wholeness is our divine inheritance. It is not what we *have* but what *has us* that enables us to embrace life completely.

Getting Our Attention

Imbalance, incongruity, ignorance, and self-deception drive the challenges of our lives. Conflicts arise to get our attention and to help us find our center and a way back to wholeness. When we push life away, however, we push against the balancing mechanism of life itself. Whether we like it or not, we must eventually meet ourselves full circle by blending the energies of our soul and our human nature into a synergistic whole. This means we must learn how to embrace life completely, without needing it to be a certain way, so we can discover that our essence cannot be limited or contained by our human experience. We must know our own innate worth, not as it is mirrored by external standards or measures, but in our own ability to be the avenue for God's expression. And most important, we must find a way to feel complete, even in our seeming brokenness.

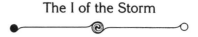

A W A R E – A P Y

1. What is the difference between the statements "Life happens to me" and "Life happens through me"?
2. Consider the thought "Only those who can see the invisible can do the impossible." Imagine that you are called to do something that is humanly impossible. What in the invisible would you need to be able to see in order to accomplish the task?
3. Make a list of all the things you don't know. How okay are you with this list? And is it really necessary that you know all of these things?
4. What is the truth about every situation (the one thing that you can know)?
5. Write a story about a situation where you did something funny or embarrassing based upon misperception.
6. Consider the idea "I have experiences, but experiences don't have me." Journal what comes to mind and note any aha's.
7. What does it mean to give your power away to a situation?

CHAPTER THREE

Enemy Mine

THE BELIEF THAT SOMEONE or something is against you is what Jesus called the "enemy." Your enemy could be your body, an illness or physical condition. Your enemy could be a dreaded eventuality such as death or a divorce. Your enemy could be an unsympathetic co-worker or a colleague who challenges your authority. Whatever seems to be against you is *your* enemy. You know that you are in relationship to an "enemy" when your first inclination is to be in control of the situation or to be right or to make the other person wrong. When you resist change, you are face-to-face with an enemy—a situation or person holding your well-being hostage.

Remember that the enemy is a reflection of

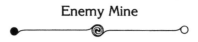

your belief that someone or something is against you. The belief is not true. Nor is it true that the person or situation is against you. Regarding the person or situation as being against you will only create more separation. You must relate differently to the experience in order to dismantle the belief that supports the experience of an enemy in your life.

What Reward Hath Ye?

In the Sermon on the Mount, Jesus told the disciples that anyone could love those who give love in return. There is no true reward in doing only what comes naturally. But to be considered a child of God, you must love where it is the most difficult to love, because this is the way God loves. "He maketh his sun to rise on the evil and on the good, and sendeth rain on the just and on the unjust" (Mt. 5:45 KJV). In other words, you must treat your enemy as you would treat a beloved friend, if you are to claim your wholeness and worth. This doesn't mean that you should put up with abuse or acquiesce to the demands of another. It means to relate to the person or situation authentically—not from fear, insecurity, or obligation, but from a willingness to be the avenue through which God can express. For this to occur, you must do as

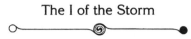

Jesus instructs: "Love your enemies, bless them that curse you, do good to them that hate you, and pray for them which despitefully use you, and persecute you" (Mt. 5:44 KJV). This instruction is a method for demonstrating your wholeness. It is also a requirement, as Jesus says, if you are to prove that you are a child of God.

Instructions on How to Deal With the Enemy

Let's look now at just how Jesus' instruction can begin to build a bridge to a consciousness of wholeness and transform the energy of *enemy* into the energy of *friend*. His instruction is a good example of shifting your awareness to the *I* of the storm. The tension between you and your enemy is the circumference—the storm. The instruction is how to move to your center, where you can be present to the enemy without feeling diminished.

To *love* means to accept, to embrace, to value. To *bless* means to endow something or someone with the capacity to be good in your life. To *do good* means to do the right thing. To *pray* means to give your thoughts to God. It's a four-step process toward your center—love, bless, do good, and pray.

1. Look Into the Mirror: Love

First, love. In the presence of the "enemy"—whoever or whatever seems to be against you—think of the person or situation as a mirror of that place in you where you are not connected to your wholeness and worth. If you were connected, you could not be intimidated or threatened. Do you see that? Now see the experience as a necessary ingredient of your own journey toward wholeness. You feel uneasy because you are not connected to your wholeness. What *inner resource* are you lacking that, if possessed instead of insecurity or fear, would enable you to relate to the person or situation as not being a threat? Is this inner resource self-confidence or personal power? What do you need that is missing from your own internal storehouse of personal resources and would allow you to be in the situation without being intimidated by it?

So now can you see that the real issue is not about the person who stands before you? It is really about what's missing in your capacity to relate to the person from a place of wholeness and worth. The person or situation is not against you, at least not insofar as being an obstacle to your highest good. The person or situation is actually *for you,* mirroring the part of you that is not connected to your wholeness and worth. So embrace the person or the situation by allowing either to be a part of your experience

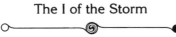

without needing anyone or anything to change or go away. Next, *value* the relationship. It offers you the opportunity to grow in awareness and discover your wholeness.

2. Make It Mean That It's for Good: Bless

Next, bless the person or situation. A blessing is something that you not only speak out loud but also think to yourself about the experience. To bless someone or something is to endow that person or thing with the capacity to be a source of good in your life. You make it mean good by speaking kindly of the person or circumstance. Like Joseph, who fell victim to his jealous brothers, you can know this: That which man has meant for evil, God has meant for good.

Blessing your enemy helps you dismantle the belief that the enemy is against you—that anything can come between you and your highest good. Your enemy is simply a mirror to that place inside yourself where you are not connected to God. Because this is the Truth, your blessing the enemy allows you to reclaim your power and dignity. The act of blessing is an expression of your faculty of faith. It places you and all concerned under the protective mantle of God. Your blessing is an affirmation that all things are working together for good.

3. Do the Right Thing: Do Good

You must work for good in the situation; that way, you are working as God is working. *Doing good* means doing the right thing. The enemy is also mirroring what is missing in your relationship. If someone is critical of you, his or her criticism is an attempt to get you to look at the relationship, or to see how you have shared in creating the problems to begin with.

The last thing you probably want to do when someone treats you badly is to do good. His or her contempt is all the evidence you need to substantiate your need to protect yourself. In order to shift from defensiveness to doing something that is an outward demonstration of spiritual maturity, you must know the Truth. No one is against you. This person's hatred is not about you. It's about what's missing in your relationship. It's about what you said or did, or didn't say or do. Or it's about what's missing in this person's attempt to find love and peace. Your purpose in this relationship is to find a greater sense of wholeness and worth and to be the avenue through which God's love flows into the relationship.

Doing the right thing means that you let go of needing to be right and focus your attention on what you can do to demonstrate your wholeness and worth in this relationship. When you feel threatened, your natural tendency is to protect yourself. You do this by needing to be right and by making your enemy wrong. This keeps you stuck in the belief that someone can be against you. It distances you from your own wholeness and worth. When you are connected to your wholeness, do you need to be right? Do you need to make the other person wrong?

Jesus said, "Unless your righteousness exceeds that of the scribes and Pharisees, you will never enter the kingdom of heaven" (Mt. 5:20 RSV). What is the righteousness of the scribes and Pharisees? "I'm right; you're wrong." The righteousness that exceeds this standard is this: "Your way is right for you; my way is right for me."

Humanly, it is impossible to be right without making someone else wrong. That is why you must shift into the question *What is the right thing to do in this situation?* The right thing to do is not about winning, defeating the enemy, or looking good. It's about taking authentic action regarding what's missing in the relationship. It's about taking ownership of how you have shared in creating the present circumstances, and it's about being responsible for the mistakes you may have made in your efforts to protect or defend yourself.

You may have every "good" reason why you'd like to prove the other person wrong, why your efforts to defend yourself are justified. You may believe yourself to be the victim in the re-

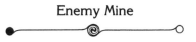

lationship, and therefore "right" in assuming that your adversary is obligated to you in some way. Indeed, no one takes offense to justice being done in circumstances of true oppression, persecution, or inequality. However, the burden is upon you to determine what actions are in alignment with your own journey toward wholeness. Jesus said, "What is a man profited, if he shall gain the whole world, and lose his own soul?" (Mt. 16:26 KJV) Being justified, right, or entitled to exacting reciprocity may come at the expense of your own wholeness and worth.

You do not lose anything by doing the right thing. It may not give you as much satisfaction as proving someone wrong; however, your reward is a true treasure in heaven.

4. Set Yourself and Your Enemy Free: Pray
The fourth step in dealing with a condition, situation, or person as your enemy is prayer. Pray for those who spitefully use you or persecute you.

You may feel like a victim in the presence of your enemy. If this is true, then your prayers are likely attempts to free yourself from the relationship or the situation. If this is the case, it is important to remember that the relationship or situation is not against you. It is for you. It is there to gift you—inviting you to embrace your wholeness and worth.

Prayer helps you fill in the gaps in your

awareness of God's presence and purpose in the situation. Praying for your enemies is a way to shift your attention to your center, your spiritual identity, so you can see the relationship as an opportunity for healing and growth.

When Jesus was on the cross, he prayed for his enemies. "Father, forgive them; for they know not what they do" (Lk. 23:34 KJV). Jesus prayed the prayer of forgiveness as a way of freeing himself of judgment and condemnation, and any sense that he was a victim. It was also a prayer that freed his enemies of the belief that they could act against him. Jesus' prayer for forgiveness shifted his entire consciousness to his center, the energy of wholeness, from which he could release any human thought of limitation, fear, or bondage. His resurrection was possible because forgiveness redeemed the atrocities visited upon him and freed those whose actions were motivated by fear and separation.

When you pray for your enemies, you move your attention to your spiritual center, where you can experience your oneness with God and your oneness with those who appear separate from you. At the center of the storm, your enemy is not against you, but for you. You are not a victim, but a victor. Prayer helps you align your thoughts and feelings, and gives you an opportunity to forgive yourself and others. When you

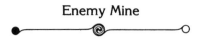

pray for your enemies, you lift yourself and the situation into the peace and serenity of God.

Like the enemy, the energy of victim gets its power from the belief that someone or something is against you. While your hurts and woundedness may seem to be evidence to the contrary, as a spiritual being, you know that the victim and abuser poles of man's inhumanity are effects of the sense of separation. If you can truly see that your suffering and ills are consequences of not being connected to your wholeness and worth, you will dismantle your defensive-reactive lifestyle and rebuild a conscious connection to the energy of Spirit. When situations arise that appear challenging, you will innately know that you are not diminished by what is before you, but strengthened by the Truth that with God all things are possible.

A W A R E – A P Y

1. Fold a piece of paper into thirds. At the top of the first
   column, write **"Body."** In the middle column, write
   "People." In the third column, write **"Life Situations."**
   Under each heading, make a list of your enemies.
   For instance, if you dislike your weight, then note
   "fat" or "overweight" as your enemy in the "Body"
   column. Do the same for "People" and "Life Situations."
2. For each enemy listed, consider how you might apply
   Jesus' instruction to love, bless, do good, and pray for
   your enemies. Use your imagination and write a
   brief statement about how it might look to love, bless,
   do good, and pray for each enemy.
3. Look at your list and pick an enemy with the least
   emotional energy attached to it. Make a commitment
   to actually follow through with Jesus' instruction. For
   extra credit, commit to embracing each enemy on
   your list.
4. Make a drawing that illustrates the difference between needing to be right and doing the right thing.

CHAPTER FOUR

Making Friends With Conflict

WHETHER YOUR CHALLENGE is with a person or a difficult situation, the tendency to avoid conflict only makes matters worse. Most of us hate to fight. We'd rather run and hide. That was my way of dealing with conflict when I was young. I had gotten into the habit of taking the long way home from school, cutting through an alley behind Safeway to avoid my nemesis Ricky, who made it his purpose to beat me up if I didn't give him money. Whenever he caught me, he'd get me in a headlock and choke me until I either cried or gave in.

One day I made a promise to myself that the next time Ricky caught me I would hold my ground. It wasn't long before Ricky surprised me, shoving me to the ground. He had been hiding

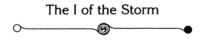
behind a trash bin, waiting for me. "Give it up, Babyface," Ricky taunted.

As I picked myself up, I saw the uneventful twelve years of my life flash before my eyes. I thought to myself, I'm not going to run. At that moment, something came over me. I hit Ricky squarely in the eye with my fist. I stood there frozen as Ricky's hands folded over his face. He fell to his knees in agony and began to cry. I soon came to my senses and ran home as fast as I could. I dashed up the stairs to my room and slammed the door behind me. I buried my head under my pillow and sobbed. Fighting felt just as bad as running. I have never forgotten how bad I felt for hurting Ricky.

Discovering the Power Within

I once had a young student testing for his first-degree black belt in tae kwon do. It was my custom to ask those testing to tell me what it meant to them to become a black belt. "The black belt," I explained, "has no power of its own. It can't protect you or help you get good grades in school. What does it symbolize?" Scott, a nine-year-old, said: "Before I became a black belt, if someone pushed me around, I either ran away or had to fight because I was afraid. Now that I am a black belt, if someone wants to fight, *I can walk away*."

I admired Scott for his insight. He helped me understand what I lacked so long ago when Ricky seemed so monstrous. I didn't know how to feel my fear and be connected to my center at the same time. That's why I ran. That's why I hit Ricky. Scott discovered a distinction between being in a threatening situation and feeling afraid, and being in the same situation and feeling confident. He didn't need to fight, because his training taught him how to be connected to his sense of well-being and wholeness. Our school motto was "Discover the Black Belt Within You," inspired by the Unity classic *Discover the Power Within You* by Eric Butterworth.[1] Scott's martial arts practice helped him discover a power within himself that was greater than his fears. He learned that fear forces action, while centeredness and confidence reveal choices and options. In spite of his youthfulness, he discovered that his true strength was rooted in defenselessness. He could walk away from a fight because fighting was rooted in fear.

The Power of Defenselessness

Long ago in feudal China, there lived a compassionate and wise Zen master named Manin-

---

[1] Eric Butterworth, *Discover the Power Within You* (New York: Harper & Row, 1968).

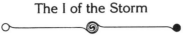

dra. His mountain home was host to many travelers and students of the Way, including the abbots and monks of neighboring monasteries. Throughout the land, he was known as a soul of unfathomable courage and presence.

One day, news came to Manindra's village that Khan, a fierce and savage Mongol warrior, was making his way across the country, attacking villages and monasteries in his path, killing anyone who showed the slightest resistance to his reign of terror. Knowing Khan's particular hatred for holy men, the people of Manindra's village begged him to hide.

Manindra, though he appreciated the concern of his followers and friends, waited at the village square for Khan's arrival. Days later, Khan stormed the village gates. To his amazement, all had fled for safety—all but Manindra, who sat motionless in the afternoon sun. Infuriated by Manindra's defiance, Khan dismounted his horse, drew his sword, and placed the blade at Manindra's chest. "Don't you know, old man," growled Khan, "I could run you through without even blinking an eye?" Manindra, centered and serene, spoke directly, "And, sir, don't you know that I could be run through without even blinking an eye?" In an astonishing moment, Khan lowered his blade and bowed at Manindra's feet, begging to be accepted as a disciple.

This story illustrates how it is possible to be wholly present to threatening circumstances and

still triumph. As difficult as it is to understand how defenselessness works to neutralize a would-be attacker, it may be even more astonishing to learn that defenselessness is at the heart of living from wholeness.

The Tao of Conflict

To give up being defensive in the presence of a threat is not easy. Something must change in *how you see the situation and what you make it mean*. The first step in making friends with conflict is in understanding what conflict is so the energy of conflict can be directed into positive avenues of understanding, healing, and spiritual growth.

Simply defined, conflict is "an interference pattern of energies."[2] It arises as a field of influence and is evident in every dimension of life—in nature, in society, and in relationships. Wherever there is change, movement, resistance, pressure, or interaction, there exists the potential for conflict. There is nothing that is without movement, without change. Every single thing is either coming into existence, developing, decaying, or going out of existence. Change and movement are the heartbeat of the universe. When change or movement is re-

---

[2] Thomas F. Crum, *Magic of Conflict: Turning a Life of Work Into a Work of Art* (New York: Simon & Schuster Inc., 1987), p. 49.

sisted or when energy patterns intersect, shock waves are created. Like colliding ripples on a pond, interfering patterns of energy create a cascade of influences that become the substance of new creations.

The Field of Creation

Change is a part of life and the natural order of things. According to *The I Ching,* an ancient Chinese text believed to be the oldest known literary work, change is never ending and proceeds according to certain universal and observable rules. *The I Ching or Book of Changes* was one of the first great successes in ancient man's attempts to find the laws that regulate all phenomena. All events and relationships have their origins in the interaction of two opposite yet complementary forces— *yin* and *yang.* This binary system of mapping the ebb and flow of creative influences in life became a method of understanding the laws of nature and the way that humanity could attain harmony with all life.

These two poles, yin and yang, and their interaction are the substance of the phenomenal universe. Whatever name we apply to these forces—matter/energy, particle/wave— their relationship is not static, but typified by constant movement and shifting of power. To

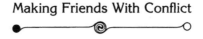

the Taoists, nothing exists of itself, but only in relation to something else. The universe is literally a dance of seeming polar opposites blending, shifting, becoming, transforming in a cosmic sea of potentiality and infinite possibilities. And while the forces of attraction and repulsion push and pull as dance partners, there is an underlying synergy that brings order to all things under heaven.

Quantum physicists have discovered an intriguing paradox common to all universal systems. As independent and isolated as we often feel we are or as separate as things appear to be, people and things exist only in relationship to all other things in the universe. There can no longer be concrete distinctions between matter and energy, particles and waves, space and time, observer and observed. Instead, there is an appreciation for a more fundamental and intrinsic quality associated with the stuff of the universe: Within all things *is* all things.

The Energy of Being and Doing

Our lives and relationships are also energetic fields subject to rules and balancing forces. Being and doing are the primary poles of self. What we do in our lives fundamentally arises out of who we are. And who we are is reinforced and made solid by what we do. In human terms, we are the energy of being and the energy of doing.

Life, as matter and energy, is the circumference. Spirit is the center. At the center there are harmony, balance, serenity, peace, and wholeness. At the circumference there are the yin and the yang, the complementary poles of energy in relationship. In the realm of Spirit, each of us is connected because there is only one Spirit. Our spirit is never in opposition to any other spirit, because Spirit is one. Depending upon where our attention is, we are either at the center or at the circumference of our lives.

Attention dictates the quality of life experience. In other words, you can be in an experience that is normally stressful or upsetting and move your attention to your center, or to Spirit, where the situation can be experienced differently. This shift in awareness is everything. When your attention moves in this manner, the nature of energy in relationship is also transformed. The movement of attention in a field of awareness creates energy. Like a magnet moving through a coil of wire, electricity is generated as the magnet influences the electrons within the conductor. In the same way, the shifting of attention within a field of infinite possibilities generates opportunities otherwise nonexistent to the observer.

Authentic Being and Conscious Doing

If the yin and yang of our energy are our being and doing, then authentic being and conscious doing allow our energies to move in the same direction as Spirit. Are you, through your intentions and desires, moving in the same direction as your Spirit? Or are you caught up in needing life to be a certain way in order to feel okay about yourself? When what we do is rooted in fear or feelings of inadequacy, we are not moving in the direction of Spirit.

You move in the same direction as Spirit when you live out of your authentic Self. Authenticity supports right action and ownership of your creative process. Have you ever not spoken your truth in order not to hurt someone or in order to get someone to like you? We do this all the time. Think of the last time someone asked you how you were feeling or doing. You probably answered, "Just fine." What if you didn't feel okay, or what if things were really terrible? Would you tell the truth? Or how about a situation where you feel betrayed by a trusted friend? Do you test the friendship by speaking your mind? You can readily see how conflict is connected to issues of authenticity when you look at the ways you may have compromised your own principles in order to please someone else—or not displease someone.

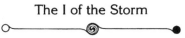

God needs you to be who you really are, because who you are is what makes you real. Your likes and dislikes, your needs and desires, and your hopes and dreams all play into how God effectively works through you to be a Presence in your life and in the lives of those you touch.

Authentic being leads to conscious doing. Conscious doing comes out of who you are as the expression of God. If what you do is not connected to the intention to serve God, it is not conscious; it is conditioned. In other words, for some activity to be considered conscious, it must be related to your spiritual purpose and living out of that intention. If you are not doing that which is the intention of the universe to fulfill itself through you as the expression of God, whatever that looks like in the context of your authentic Self, then what you do is not conscious doing, but conditioned doing.

When the poles of being and doing become imbalanced (out of integrity) or conflicted, an interference pattern of energies arises and creates tension and stress in your life. You can readily see how much conflict is created in relationships when you are unable, for whatever reason, to speak your truth. You may not always know how you feel about a particular issue in the moment, but you usually know when you have acquiesced against your better judgment.

Regret is often a symptom of not being authentic in relation to a particular circumstance. When you fail to speak your truth or act in integrity with your own values and guiding principles, you experience a measure of torment. While you may have difficulty in defining your own sense of authenticity, you are acutely aware when you are not being true to yourself.

Not speaking our truth is a strategy most of us learned as children. We all have been raised to blend in to some degree, or not feel our feelings. It is no wonder that so many of us have become codependent in our relationships. We have found greater security and comfort in meeting other people's needs, responding to other people's feelings rather than our own. Authenticity is a fundamental component of wholeness. It honors all that we are. With authenticity, we become cocreators of a fulfilling life that springs forth from all which is genuine and beautiful in us. Authenticity is the litmus test of our self-worth. When we truly value ourselves, we live in integrity with our spiritual nature.

Authentic being and conscious doing are the quintessential nature of self. It could be said that authentic being and conscious doing are the energy of individuality and the field within which we express our wholeness. When we are true to our principles and values and when we value others and ourselves, our energy field is dynamic and filled with potential. But when we have our being and doing mixed up—when we need to be right instead of doing the right thing, for instance—our energy field is discordant. Discord produces disharmony and sets interfering patterns of energy in motion. In time, every energy pattern comes back to its source.

Conflict Brings Us to the Edge

Conflict brings us to the edge of our resourcefulness. That is why the idea of embracing conflict feels so unnatural, even frightening. One of the most uncomfortable feelings is not knowing what to do or how to be when a situation looks and feels scary. Conflict is *conflict* because we don't know how to relate to a perceived threat in a way that enables us to feel safe and okay. When this happens, the well of our resourcefulness seems to run dry.

Linda, a shy and insecure junior executive of an investment firm, hated her job, but felt obligated to endure its drudgery because she needed the money. She often felt threatened by her boss. His manner was abrupt and condescending. One day she inadvertently offended a client, who demanded that she be fired. Her boss, as expected, accused her of incompetence and demanded that she appease the client and

do whatever it took to get the account back. The enormity of the situation caused Linda to retreat into despair. She feared losing her job and the security it provided, but even more, she dreaded the prospect of meeting face-to-face the person who had it in for her.

The situation placed Linda at the edge of her resourcefulness. She didn't feel safe. She didn't know what to do or how she could possibly manage the meeting with the client. She knew her boss would be there, looming over her shoulder, ready to cut her loose the moment she failed to make it right.

Linda realized that this was not the first time she had felt threatened or in a situation which seemed overwhelming. The situation was reminiscent of two failed marriages that brought her to a similar crossroad in her search for wholeness. She knew the pattern well, knew that beneath the details which made this situation unique, the same story was unfolding. She was searching for a missing piece. She was missing a connection to her own wholeness.

Moments before her meeting she prayed for strength. She asked God, "What resource do I need in order to be in this experience without feeling diminished?" It occurred to her that what she was missing was a true appreciation of her own worth. She remembered a time when she saved a boy's life in a house fire and how grateful the child's parents were for her heroic efforts. She reflected on this and other occasions when she knew her presence mattered and when she had made a difference in others' lives.

As she entered the meeting room, Linda took a leap of faith off the edge of her adversity. She demanded an apology from the client for his insensitivity and from her boss for his lack of appreciation and trust in her abilities. Not only did she stand up for herself, Linda gave herself what she had always sought from others—affirmation. And while she lost her job, not only did she gain a real connection to her own dignity, she moved on to discover her passion for community service and became a paramedic.

It is important to remember, however, that conflict does not come to us, it comes *from* us. It arises from within as an effect of two competing intentions: a compelling desire to feel safe, okay, and valued, and the drive to fulfill the soul's purpose.

The soul's purpose is to bring one into the fullness of being as a creation of God in those areas of life where that is not happening. Therefore, the soul's intention lives out of the Spirit of God. The soul's top priority is to bring one into relationship with those aspects of self that live outside of wholeness and a sense of authentic being. This often happens when we enter into relationships with the kinds of individuals

or experiences that threaten us the most. We are afraid because we don't feel safe—we don't see God at our point of experience.

When we realize that this inherent conflict between one's soul and one's human nature plays out in daily life, we will see that what appears as an adversary in life is really a mirror of one's own resistance. Our resistance and defensiveness, therefore, arise out of those parts of ourselves that are not connected to our wholeness. How else is it possible to feel threatened or afraid? We can only have these feelings because some part is not connected to the Truth of our being.

The Soul's Conspiracy

The soul seeks to move one into those areas of life where full potential has yet to be discovered. Imagine that you are overly dependent upon another person as a source of approval or appreciation. This dependency would naturally block the knowing of your own innate worth. However, when you are ready to take greater ownership of the possibilities that live within you, circumstances may arise to change the relationship. Relationship changes that threaten your sense of security are almost always resisted. Yet your soul and the souls of those who journey with you have conspired to help you

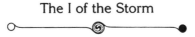

gain freedom. The word *conspire* comes from the Latin. It means "to breathe together." In effect, you are breathing together with others the intention to move into a more authentic expression of God. Conflict helps motivate you.

Whatever is going on in your life is there to bring you into greater alignment with the Truth of who you are. If who you really are is a worthy and talented person, then every time you discount yourself or settle for less than your highest good, you are setting yourself up for upset. Your life situations and emotional responses can give you insight into those parts that are not connected to your true Selfhood.

Opportunity Over Danger

The renowned psychiatrist Carl G. Jung, in a passionate forward to The I Ching or Book of Changes,[3] gives testimony to the extraordinary accuracy and wisdom of the ancient oracle. As an archetypal guide to the human psyche or as a template for discerning the movement of the universe, the Book of Changes offers insight into the nature of conflict.

In the Book of Changes, Hexagram 6 is made up of two primary forces, heaven and the abyss,

---

[3] Richard Wilhelm and Cary F. Baynes (translators), *The I Ching or Book of Changes* (Princeton, New Jersey: Princeton University Press, 1981).

which describe the energy of conflict. The symbols heaven (Spirit) and the abyss (water) denote the nature of conflict. The abyss is symbolic of coming to a place (internal or external) of great trepidation. At the abyss, we lack the skills, confidence, awareness, or the resources to manage a situation. We stand at an edge, where we are face-to-face with our fears and the unknown. The darkness of the watery pit mirrors our insecurities and deficiencies. The abyss appears intent upon swallowing us up.

Yet it is at this very edge that we discover what we are really made of. Our doubts and insecurities reveal themselves—not as weaknesses, but as areas of potentiality. It is because we are on journeys that our quests are sometimes perilous. Our willingness to look into the abyss places us at the edge of awakening. It is in the face of danger that we either do or die. And when forced to confront our fears, our only recourse is to step into the abyss, to surrender and let go. Conflict leads to rebirth and transformation. It is only in the presence of challenging circumstances that we awaken to the possibilities of the moment. Because heaven is the realm of infinite possibilities, danger forces us to break new ground, to discover latent resources. Conflict stretches us, forcing us at times to adapt, to learn, or to yield.

When Nicodemus asked Jesus about the kingdom of God, he answered him, "Truly, truly, I say to you, unless one is born anew, he cannot see the kingdom of God" (Jn. 3:3 RSV). Puzzled by this saying, Nicodemus questioned Jesus: "How can a man be born when he is old?" (Jn. 3:4 RSV) Jesus replied, "I say to you, unless one is born of water and the Spirit, he cannot enter the kingdom of God" (Jn. 3:5 RSV). Nicodemus understood the symbols water and Spirit. Water represents cleansing, baptism, and purification. Spirit literally means breath, the life force. A spiritual and water rebirth brings us into relationship with those parts of ourselves that have yet to be integrated into our senses of wholeness and well-being. Our fears, false beliefs, judgments, and limitations live in us as a watery pit, the abyss. Conflict is our spiritual midwife. Through cleansing and purification, we breathe new life into our being. We awaken to possibilities that only conflict can reveal to us.

Conflict brings us into relationship with the kingdom of God, the dimension of life that is pure potentiality. We do not readily open ourselves to challenging circumstances without certain assurances. Our need to feel safe and okay about ourselves moves us away from the abyss. Yet it is at those very edges where we experience being most alive.

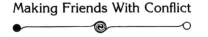

Embrace Tiger/Return to Mountain

There is an ancient Chinese saying—"embrace tiger/return to mountain"—from the martial art tai chi chuan that suggests a methodology for managing conflict. If to "return to mountain" is synonymous with equanimity, peace, and harmony, the ancients believed that it could only be realized by becoming present to life, by embracing the "tigers" that crossed one's path. This makes a lot of spiritual sense. But when it comes down to putting it into practice, everything in us wants to do just the opposite. The instinctive response to a perceived threat is to run, fight, or freeze—not embrace. After all, we know what it feels like to be chewed on, scratched, and eaten up by the "tigers" in our lives. Most of us have scars or deep wounds from past run-ins with the crafty beasts. The idea of making friends with conflict seems so unnatural, given the world in which we live. How do we override the tendency to push away what looks and feels bad? How do we become present to circumstances when we don't feel safe or okay about ourselves? How do we embrace the tiger and return to the mountain? The answer lies in knowing our wholeness and worth.

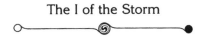

Resistance Is Futile!

If your soul is a force within you that seeks to push you toward ever-increasing levels of spiritual growth and development, then your resistance to this pressure is what produces discomfort, stress, and ultimately the storm. When you resist the movement of Spirit, you create friction, heat, and conflict. When you struggle with conditions that challenge or threaten you, you invariably reinforce their presence in your life.

Resistance as an electrical principle is a metaphor for the way conflict arises when aspects of your being get in the way of God's expression. Resistance, in electrical terminology, is the property of conductivity of an electrical conductor. According to Ohm's law of resistance, the amount of current flow through an electrical conductor is inversely proportional to the amount of resistance in the wire. This means that when resistance is high, current flow is low. Conversely, when resistance approaches zero, current flow approaches infinity.

If you consider your consciousness to be a medium through which divine ideas flow, the factors that limit this flow can be called resistance. Since consciousness is both a creative force and the mediator of your life experience, your perceptions and awareness can function simi-

larly to resistance, if they are limiting. For instance, a belief in lack blocks the flow of abundance into your life. Feelings of unworthiness or inadequacy keep you from experiencing love and fulfillment. As you can see, resistance in consciousness can be in the form of thoughts, feelings, or beliefs.

Resistance narrows the path through which the energy of being travels. It manifests itself in consciousness as the tendency to push away what feels bad or to hold on to what feels good. Resistance is a conditioned aspect of consciousness that has become integrated into your defense mechanisms and coping strategies.

Outer Resistance

Resistance manifests itself in two dimensions, outer resistance and inner resistance. In either case, we are both the object and the source of resistance.

Outer resistance is experienced as external opposition to your movement or intention to move. A physical limit, an opposing opinion, or a judgment can be a form of outer resistance. It feels as if something is "in your way" or against you. Traffic jams, a rain shower on opening day of the playoffs, or an unforeseen circumstance are examples of outer resistance, as well. In each case, there is the tendency to push the situation away or to wish things were different. This "wishing things were different" takes you out of the moment and gives power to the situation. Reacting to a judgment or criticism does the same thing. Something you said or did may have offended a friend or a coworker. His or her reprimand (outer resistance) may seem spiteful and condescending. You become defensive in the presence of someone's reaction. The resistance feels like an attack, and you resist in turn. Outer resistance becomes a problem when you personalize the resistance and make what resists you your adversary.

Outer resistance is useful as feedback to your creative process. When someone resists you—judges you, let's say—he or she opposes your *doing*. Something you have said or done has drawn resistance. You benefit from this resistance because it gives you a chance to review your intentions and creative process. If someone finds fault with what you have said or done, that person's reaction gives you a chance to choose to correct the situation, make amends if necessary, or stand by your actions and take responsibility for them. If, instead, you become defensive when someone takes offense with what you said or did, you become compelled to make the other person wrong. Making someone wrong damages your relationship with the person and creates conflict.

Outer resistance not only teaches you how people perceive you, it helps make you stronger and more flexible and willing to look at life and people differently. When you embrace resistance, rather than push it away, you make resistance your ally and advisor. Outer resistance becomes the basis of finding common ground and mutuality. When you disagree but are willing to discover what is underlying the disagreement, you strengthen the relationship. You make the issue be about what's missing in the relationship or what each individual needs, instead of who is right or wrong. Intimacy, trust, and cohesiveness grow in relationships as resistance is embraced and transformed into appreciation.

It is possible to embrace outer resistance because outer resistance is never about *you*. Someone's judgment is not about *you*. No one is really ever against *you*. It is impossible for anyone to oppose *you*. Outer resistance is about what you said or did, what the relationship needs, or what the other person needs, but it is never about *you*. Outer resistance is about who you are *not*—your unclarity, your misperception, your driven behavior, your ego, or your pretense. It is never about you, the *real* you. Resisting resistance only makes more concrete who you are not.

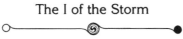

Inner Resistance

Inner resistance is a defensive posture assumed when life is experienced as a direct assault upon one's well-being. It is characterized by reactive behaviors, justifications, prejudices, and the need to be right. It creates a tension around future possibilities. Pushing easily becomes shoving. Your discomfort or anxiety concerning the situation compels you to action. You feel unsafe and threatened. Inner resistance triggers the fight/flight response. It is your first line of defense when the situation is perceived as adversarial.

Inner resistance keeps you from being present to life and to those you perceive as a threat. It causes your energy field to contract; you move away instead of closer. Inner resistance reinforces your belief about the situation or person. It becomes the basis for how you justify your actions. If you perceive me as a threat, you will use your own experience of defensiveness as evidence that I am against you. Your resistance and defensiveness are proof that I must be out to hurt you. Inner resistance separates you from your spiritual resources and intuition. It confuses the line between you and your experience.

Many years ago, when I first set out to open a martial arts school, my lofty plans for success were derailed when a new school opened across

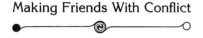

town. As competitive as martial artists tend to be among themselves, the rivalry between competing schools often hinges upon the prominence and notoriety of the schools' chief instructors. Like neighborhood kids pitting their dads against each other, my students indulged fantasies of me karate chopping and spinning back kicking my opponent into bankruptcy.

If the truth were known, Master Edwards made attempts to establish an alliance with me when he first moved into town. But because I saw him as a threat, I mistook his overtures as suspicious. I projected upon him my own insecurities and fears. I used these feelings to substantiate a defensive relationship to someone who genuinely sought to create a mutually beneficial relationship.

The important point to see about resistance is that it arises from within. While it appears to be triggered by external conditions, resistance surfaces from within and keeps you from being present to the moment. This becomes a major factor in creating conflict because it works against your soul's intention. Your soul moves you toward the present moment so you can take authentic action. When you are driven to avoid a situation by resisting it, you fail to get the gift that the situation offers.

Thus inner resistance functions in consciousness as an attribute of being. "I am resis-

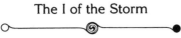

tant" or "I am resisted" each creates its counter-part in the form of life situations. "I am resistant" creates an energetic force field around you. It says that you are not present, you are not re-sponsible, you are not safe. "I am resisted" re-inforces the perception of separation and the belief that someone is against you.

Because resistance in consciousness is a con-ditioned phenomenon that takes you out of the present moment, the process of managing re-sistance, and thereby the circumstances that mir-ror resistance, lies in addressing conditioned be-liefs and their attending behaviors. Conditioned beliefs persist in consciousness because they are reinforced by conditioned responses. This feedback loop is weakened when you become *present* to a situation that routinely causes de-fensiveness and when you can respond to it authentically.

Resisting the Resistance

Resistance, in and of itself, is not the prob-lem. As a matter of fact, resistance is necessary and useful. The application of electrical prin-ciples can only occur when the properties of resistance are reconciled with the design and the intention of the electrical application. Our physical and psychological growth and devel-opment would be impossible if there were no

resistance. Resistance, challenge, and conflict are necessary elements in our lives because these conditions stretch us and cause us to discover new dimensions within one another and ourselves.

The problem with resistance is that we personalize it. We take it as evidence that something is wrong. Because resistance produces friction, heat, and difficulty at the beginning, it becomes something that we want to avoid. Conflict is most acutely the effect of *resisting the resistance.*

A W A R E - A P Y

1. Think of a relationship that failed. Consider how not being authentic, real, or honest contributed to its demise. What underlying beliefs do you have about yourself that support the patterns of your life?

2. Identify some of the abysses you have faced in your life. What opportunities did you also discover?

3. For this exercise you will need a large sheet of newsprint and a crayon or colored marker. You are going to draw a single unbroken line across the paper, as if tracing your life's journey. You will start from the left and move to the right side of the paper. In this exercise you are going to make a map of the resistances you have encountered along your way. Bring to mind some of the major challenges you remember facing. Your line will turn left or right, up or down, at each encounter of some obstacle. So in other words, your line will start out straight and then change direction in order to negotiate the particular life circumstance that showed up as resistance in your life. Your line will resume course across the page after you have either gone around the obstacle or somehow circumvented it. It's like tracing a line through a maze or labyrinth puzzle without the walls. You will mentally project the walls (resistances) onto your

map. The finished drawing will probably look like a trek through a maze, with the exception that you are going from one side of the paper to the other.

4. Go back to your drawing and label each obstacle by identifying the situation and noting your feelings associated with the experience. What do you notice about your journey? Does the resistance you draw in your life have a theme? Has resistance in your life made you stronger and wiser?

CHAPTER FIVE

The Four Winds of Conflict

Now let's look at the conditions that support the storm which is conflict. I call them "the four winds of conflict." By now you understand that conflict in your life is evidence of not being fully present or authentic in a particular situation or relationship. It does not arise in a vacuum, and it does not have a single cause. Certain conditions must exist to give rise to conflict. When these conditions exist, the likelihood of conflict increases. Conflict is the effect of a complex array of influences.

It is useful to identify the conditions that support the presence of conflict the same way it is useful to forecast the potential threat of a developing weather system. Knowing how conflict arises, what supports its presence, and what

factors contribute to its intensification will help you make shifts in how you relate to the issues at hand. The *four winds* or conditions that support the storm are: *separation, misperception, competition,* and *defensiveness.* While these conditions often exist in most relationships, they don't necessarily result in supporting conflict. The pivotal component in the conflict equation is how you feel about yourself. When you are tired, hungry, angry, lonely, or depressed, the factors that support conflict are accentuated. Being on edge and feeling insecure or unsure of yourself are also contributing factors. You are susceptible to conflict much in the same way you are susceptible to getting a cold or an infection. When your stress level is high and your immune system is weak, the likelihood of breakdowns increases.

The Sense of Separation

Unless your parents were Mary and Joseph, you were probably never told that you are a child of God. You were unable to know your true Self as whole and perfect. You were born into a world system that was unable to mirror your innate worth to a degree which would allow you to emerge into adulthood with your sense of wholeness intact. Your caregivers were

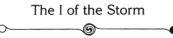

not always able to be totally present, fully alive, to you. When you needed their presence, whether in the form of love or protection, and they were not able to be there for you, the impact of those moments caused you to separate from your original state of wholeness. During the first two years of life, over a span of innumerable impressionable moments, you learned that sometimes it wasn't good to be connected. Separation was a way of avoiding the pain of being too close, too vulnerable, and too innocent. Eventually you adopted core assumptions and beliefs about yourself and about the nature of life. You had no way of understanding or explaining the painful moments of your life, so you blamed yourself for the neglect and abuse you may have experienced.

The sense of separation you feel within yourself, between others, and in life generally is an *effect* of being born into an imperfect caregiving environment. Rebirth into this world subjected you to events and circumstances that caused you to separate yourself from your essential wholeness. In order to manage a separate existence, you have learned how to control others, avoid conflict, resist change, and be right. By being right, you circumvented the pain of your past—memories of those moments when what you needed most was to be loved but you got instead an experience that taught you it sometimes hurts to be connected, de-

pendent, and innocent. To manage this imperfect world, you learned how to separate yourself, first, from experiences; then, from others; then, from yourself; and then, from God.

Your adaptations from early childhood created a lifestyle of defensiveness and the need for life to be a certain way in order to feel secure, safe, or okay about yourself. You moved from being connected to being separate, and then to being codependent. You don't have a clue as to your worth or well-being without first having to look outside yourself for evidence. When you need me to be a certain way in order for you to feel okay about yourself, you are codependent.

Codependence creates a heightened sensitivity toward the actions and motives of others. You become highly vested in outcomes. You learn how to manipulate and control people and situations in order to manage your fears. It inevitably creates conflict because it leads to ever greater dependence upon others for what is missing in you.

Codependence can be seen as a "depend dance" that binds you to what is happening in your life. Your life dances around issues of what's happening to you. You *depend* upon situations or relationships being a certain way, as if the way things are is the measure of your well-being and worth.

Codependence is an inappropriate reliance

upon *what's happening* as the context for knowing our wholeness and worth. This is not to say
that we shouldn't be dependent upon others.
Needing someone's assistance or support is not
codependence. We need others and we need
situations to work out for the best. The problem
is when we become diminished by what happens or by how things are. If this can happen,
then dependence separates us from an authentic connection field of infinite possibilities.

Another important aspect of codependence
is how it affects a person's willingness to take
responsibility for his or her experiences. Codependence places the burden of one's well-being
on the performance of someone else. When conflict arises due to the tension created by this
type of relationship, the tendency is for the dependent person to blame the other for the dependent's disappointment or upset. As blame
intensifies, the capacity for people to take responsibility for their experiences diminishes.

The impact of being born into an imperfect
caregiving environment is the creation of a sense
of separate selfhood. In your sense of separation, you are driven to avoid what threatens
you or makes you feel unsafe. You do this by
trying to control others and by making your life
mean that people or circumstances are against
you. But sooner or later you must ask yourself,
"Does controlling others, needing to be right, or

avoiding conflict really work for me?" When you can truly see that these ways of managing your life only reinforce your sense of separation and when you can also see how in your separation you create conflict, you will begin to move toward wholeness.

Your defensiveness, resistance, and need to be right are all adaptations to the human condition rooted in the imperfect caregiving environment. They are not who you really are. Do you see that? They are conditioned responses in an effort to manage an imperfect world. If you realize this, you can see that conflict is symptomatic of *miscommunion*—breakdowns or missing pieces in the intention to connect, to commune, or to cocreate. Your separation creates safety in a world of uncertainty, but also prevents your experiencing communion. When you are unable to experience communion within yourself, with others, or in life circumstances generally, you are unable to experience the presence of God. Separation supports conflict because separation keeps you from experiencing God in yourself, in others, and in life overall.

Misperception

All conflicts possess an element of misperception. When we stop and consider the mechanics of perception, we can readily appreciate

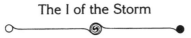

the enormous effort it takes to truly understand another person. Our capacity to accurately read a situation is influenced by how we see things, how we hear what's being said, and how okay we feel about ourselves. Anger, fear, defensiveness, and other emotional states also contribute to how we perceive a situation.

Another important factor is what psychologist Maria Nemeth terms "structures of knowing." Both our conscious and our unconscious awarenesses have distinct boundaries. Within the boundaries of our awareness is everything we know—our thoughts, feelings, beliefs, facts, justifications, and so on. Outside our structures of knowing are other dimensions of reality beyond our comprehension or conscious thought. Our capacities to see, hear, and understand are limited by our structure of knowing. Dr. Nemeth describes structures of knowing as being like a fencing mask: "The grid is between you and your world."[4] Beyond the grid are possibilities that include all the missing pieces our viewing point can't grasp. The issue here is that everyone's viewing point is limited, self-serving, and fragmented.

One positive aspect of conflict is that it moves us to the edges of our structures of knowing.

---

[4] Maria Nemeth, Ph.D., *You and Money: Would It Be All Right With You if Life Got Easier?* (Sacramento, California: Vildehiya Publications, 1997), p. 132.

How else do we expand our awareness or broaden our viewing point? It forces us to step outside of our viewing point to see what lies beyond in the realm of possibilities. Conflict produces a displacement between what we know and what we don't know, between what we see and what we don't see. When individuals or communities use conflict as an opportunity to challenge their own ways of seeing things, they awaken to new aspects of themselves. They discover that their awarenesses can expand and grow beyond the limitations of their yesterday selves.

When you feel unsafe in a particular situation and investigate where the feeling of "unsafe" comes from, you will discover that this feeling is linked to how you perceive your experience. The feeling arises from what you know, believe, or imagine about the situation. Uncertainty, confusion, and paradox are the outer boundaries of your structures of knowing. Conflict inherently brings you to these outer limits in your capacity to assess your experience. This is a powerful and transformative dynamic. When we arrive at the edge of our capacity to make sense of or to define our experience, we are at the threshold of the kingdom of God, the realm of infinite possibilities.

Understanding how misperception feeds conflict is vital to working in adversarial relationships. Until people shift their viewing points, the context of their experiences doesn't change.

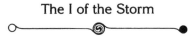

They can be shown the truth. The facts can be placed before them. But until a new frame of reference that transcends the structure of knowing is created, seeing, hearing, and understanding will remain conditioned by predominantly psychological factors. In other words, there must be a distinction drawn between *what the real problems are* and *what has become a problem because of misperception.*

Competition: Competing Needs, Goals, and Values

Between the poles of personality and circumstance, we experience the challenge to get our needs met, to achieve our goals and dreams, and to feel good about ourselves. It's easy to see that in any relationship there is a mixture of needs, wants, and priorities. When what we want, or value, gets in the way of someone else, conflict occurs.

When people experience difficulty in getting what they need and want out of their relationships, they may distance themselves from their partners. If clear and open channels of communication are absent, people will become defensive and endeavor to gain the advantage by gathering evidence to support their positions. As conflict escalates, people become competitive and motivated to win or to be right.

Eventually these methods of managing the tension of competing needs, goals, and values become a lifestyle as parties master the art of manipulation, control, and deception—the necessary strategies of winning the game.

The danger of competition in relationships is that someone must eventually lose. The loser becomes diminished, angry, and resentful. The winner loses as well because the reward for being right is the reinforcement of one's inferiority. Winning reinforces inferiority because needing to be right is a behavior that masks or protects one's sense of insecurity or inadequacy. This is unfortunate because the purpose of relationships is to be a source of support and empowerment. When this is not the case, relationships become a playing field where civility and fairness take a backseat to winning.

Think about a recent contest you may have had with a friend or a coworker. Perhaps you were competing over an issue—who's right and who's wrong. Maybe the game was about getting your partner's undivided attention or affection. If you have to compete to get what you need, you do so at the expense of your own sense of wholeness and worth. Conflict that is rooted in competing needs, goals, and values is symptomatic of people who have forgotten their purpose and who have lost their heart connection within the relationship.

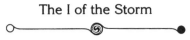

Defensiveness

Defensiveness is a psychophysical dynamic that impacts a relationship directly. When you become defensive, your entire body participates. Your energy field collapses to allow muscles to stiffen and allow reflexes to queue in response to impending danger. This energetic dynamic produces a resonance field. Imagine a pebble thrown into a still pond. As the ripples radiate outward, so does the resonance of defensiveness. Everything and everyone in your proximity is signaled. Animals feel the fear and anxiety of a passerby.

Likewise, on an unconscious level, your defensiveness will engender defensiveness in others. If someone walked into a meeting room brandishing a weapon, everyone would be frozen with fear. If, instead of a weapon, an angry attitude was projected into a discussion, you would become uneasy. Perhaps even more astonishing, your subtle shift from ease to dis-ease, from openness to defensiveness, in the presence of a real or imagined threat is projected like a beacon. When you unconsciously pick up on someone's anxiety or defensiveness, you instinctively resonate with that person's defensiveness by becoming defensive yourself.

By its very definition, defensiveness implies the presence of an adversary. It is evidence

that the situation is a potential threat to one's well-being. When a person's defenses are activated, people distance themselves from one another. They withdraw their energy. They become rigid and entrenched. Defensiveness holds the relationship hostage to the suspicions and fears of its partners. Conflict doesn't have a place to go until someone lets down his or her guard and risks coming out into the open.

Defensiveness is linked to the fight-or-flight response. This primitive survival tactic plays out in our daily lives in subtle and not so subtle ways. Each of us is conditioned to relate to conflict in a particular manner. Most are so uncomfortable with conflict that they will do almost anything to avoid it. Some people react aggressively toward a perceived threat. Their defensiveness leads them to take preemptive measures. Others may deny, minimize, or relate only superficially to interpersonal conflicts. In most cases, conditioned and instinctive methods of relating to difficult situations and people exacerbate issues and keep the level of conflict high.

Defensiveness is evidence of separation. When I am threatened and compelled to protect myself, I instinctively distance myself from my adversary. I use whatever resources I possess to manage the situation. Defensiveness can only be shunted at its root—resistance. The instant that I feel threatened or wronged, I start

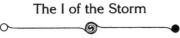

pushing away. Pushing the situation away never works. Resistance moves quickly into defensiveness and self-protection.

You Can Overcome the Forces of Conditioning

The four winds of conflict—separation, misperception, competition, and defensiveness—are interrelated and rooted in the conditioned aspects of mind. They are factors that contribute to the likelihood of interpersonal difficulty and situational challenges. While they are characteristic of the human condition and support the presence of conflict, they are held in stasis by our spiritual identities—the *I* of the storm. Because you are a spiritual being, because your wholeness *is,* you can direct your attention and awareness to your center, your spiritual Self, and bring the attributes of the center to the experience of the storm.

You Are Not Your Parts

In the next chapters we will look at the four attributes of wholeness: Communion, Principle, Purpose, and Nonresistance. First, for the moment think about yourself as being a collection of parts. Think about the part of you that loves to be creative. Think about the part of you that

dreads housework or paying the bills. Imagine the part of you which feels threatened when judged and the part of you which likes an adventure. Think about your life and how it seems to be compartmentalized. Part of you is living in a world of vocation or career. Another part is rooted in family life. Sometimes you may feel either disconnected or together, either scattered or congruent. We even think of God as having parts. There seems to be a part of God which is loving and forgiving as well as a part of God which is distant and impersonal. While we believe that God is everywhere, there seem to be places and situations where it's hard to find God.

Isn't it interesting how attention and awareness organize themselves according to patterns and associations within a context of distinctive parts? We break up our lives and ourselves into many neat and not so neat packages. Why? Partly (pardon the pun) because that is how our minds work, and partly because it is easier to deal with life if it is segmented.

In our disjointed and divided world, we naturally feel fragmented. We naturally feel incomplete. When we look inside ourselves, we notice our parts—our insecurities, fears, strong emotions, dependencies, compulsions, hurts, and regrets. We also see our strengths, talents, and passions. Yet what gets our attention is the emptiness, loneliness, and confusion we sense when part of us doesn't feel okay. When we don't feel okay about ourselves, we look outside for what seems to be missing. We look for our wholeness in terms of finding the missing parts we need in order to be complete. We look for the right person—the one who will make us happy and love us, no matter what. We look for the perfect job—the one that will give meaning to our existences. Or we look for our wholeness by trying to rid ourselves of those parts of ourselves we dislike. Either way, our efforts to fill in the gaps in the equation of our well-being rarely lead directly to wholeness. The sum of all our parts never seems to be as whole as we hoped it would be.

Imagine for a moment that you don't think of yourself as a collection of parts. In other words, imagine there is no such thing as the part of you that feels insecure. In a particular moment, you may *feel* insecure, but you are not your insecure feeling. There is a distinction between you and your feeling of insecurity. You are not your feelings. There is no such thing as a part of you that is fearful, either. You may experience fear, but the fear is not you—nor is it a part of you. There is no such thing as the part of you that wants to succeed. You may wish for a better life, but your wishing is not you. Consider the possibility that there is no such thing as the

part of you that is a lover or a parent or a friend. What if there is just *you* pouring the totality of your whole Self into a relational existence that simply has many sides—or many facets, like a finely cut gemstone?

You Are Not Your Experiences

The first step in discovering wholeness is in seeing the distinction between you and your experiences. You have experiences, but you are not your experiences. You make the mistake of seeing your experiences as your parts—like hands and feet. You have body parts, but your body parts don't have you. The reason why wholeness seems so elusive is that you base your sense of well-being and worth on what is happening or not happening to you. You confuse your experiences with yourself. You think you are not whole based upon how your life looks and feels. This keeps you looking in the wrong places for a wholeness that can only be experienced as an attribute of authentic being in the act of conscious doing.

Once it is clear to you that you are not your experiences, that experiences are the effects of the energy of being and doing, you will begin to see yourself in holistic terms. You are the energy of being and doing. Your spiritual identity or individuality is the energy of authentic being

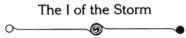

and conscious doing. Your personality and the illusion of separation are an effect of conditioned being and unconscious doing. Your wholeness supports your authentic being, moving you to conscious action. It is what God has placed at your center as the foundation of an abundant life.

A W A R E – A P Y

1. Read the parable of the dragnet, found in Matthew 13:47–50. If the kingdom of heaven represents the process of your spiritual unfolding and the good fish represent true beliefs about yourself and the bad fish represent false beliefs about yourself, then the process of separating or self-differentiating from what is true and not true about yourself is what your spiritual journey is all about. The goal is to enter the kingdom of heaven, or to mature spiritually. Consider what fish you have gathered to the shores of your life right now. What beliefs—true beliefs and false beliefs—fill your net?

2. How would your life be different if you could cast away the bad fish?

3. How close does Matthew 13:50 come to describing your struggle to separate yourself from your false-hoods? Explain.

4. Play a game of solitaire with 48 cards. How is this game similar to some of the games you might find yourself playing in life?

5. If your struggle to satisfy your emotional or intimacy needs could be described as a major league sport, what game would you be playing?

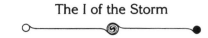

6. Think of two or three situations where you find yourself becoming defensive. Now stand in front of a
   mirror and exaggerate how you might posture yourself in each relationship. Pretend a passerby has just
   noticed you. From the passerby's vantage point, describe what he or she might be noticing about the
   scene.

CHAPTER SIX

Communion

RELATIONSHIP IS THE ARENA in which you experience your wholeness and worth. You have only one relationship—your relationship with God. Your relationship with God is experienced within three subarenas: Your relationship to life, with others, and with yourself. In each of these categories, the objective is to experience communion with God—God in life, in others, and in you.

Communion is the first attribute of wholeness. *Communion* means being connected—connected to life and to God. It also means "common union." There is a shared intention in the communion experience that transcends individuality without eclipsing it. Musicians playing together in a symphony are an example of

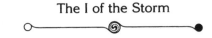

common union. Each is an essential component of the whole that moves together with purpose.

Here Comes the Judge

Communion is the *I* of the storm of separation. When you don't feel connected to someone, it's easy to find fault or become disappointed. Disagreements and relationship conflicts are symptomatic of *miscommunion*—breakdowns or missing pieces in the intention to connect. Judgment and criticism are also indicators of missing pieces—signals alerting partners that the relationship needs attention.

When you are not connected to your sense of wholeness and worth, you will misread these signals and mistakenly assume that your partner is against you. If in the instant someone judges you, you react by trying to disprove the accusation or by defending yourself, you will miss the opportunity to respond authentically to the invitation to create communion.

A few months ago my wife Nan said to me, "Gary, you *never* take me out to dinner!" Well, of course, that's not true. We go out to dinner all the time, that is, when we can agree on a restaurant we both like. But what happened was that I reacted and came up with a list of dates and places where we had, indeed, gone out to

dinner. So you see, Sweetie, I said to myself, *never* is not true.

I won the argument but I lost the opportunity to give Nan what she really wanted, which wasn't dinner, but was to feel closer to me. I had been gone for a week or so on a business trip and she missed me. It just so happened the method she used to get my attention was a judgment—*You never take me out to dinner*. When I make Nan wrong by proving myself right, not only do I reinforce the part of me that doesn't feel okay, but I also tell Nan it isn't okay for her to be needy. She gets penalized for being needy when I make her wrong. The tragic thing about her judgment is that it wasn't ever about me. It was about what was missing for her. Her judgment was simply an attempt to get my attention.

The same is true regarding every judgment. *No judgment is about you.* It is about the person who is doing the judging. But when you react by making the other person wrong or by defending yourself, you make the judgment mean that it is about you, when it's really not. It is about what is missing for the other person. It's about what the other person needs or what the relationship needs. Or it is about what you said or did (or didn't say or do) that has caused some concern. In any case, it is important that you

have this information because it gives you the chance to fill in the gaps, repair the breakdowns, and discover the missing pieces in the intention to create communion. So you see, judgments are not about you; they are *for* you.

When you react to someone's judgment, you must quickly take ownership of your reaction and defensiveness. Your reaction is not about the other person's judgment. Your reaction is about you! It's about your need to feel safe and okay. It's about your need to be right. Or it's about some unresolved issue of your past that has been triggered. In any case, you move to center by focusing upon what the relationship needs in order to create communion. Learn to value judgment and criticism as opportunities to live from your wholeness and worth.

You live from wholeness when you are connected to life. Being connected means being responsive and engaged. There is intention and purpose in each moment. Being connected to life, to others, and to yourself means embracing the moment or the situation as if *life* depended upon it. It's knowing that your presence really matters, that you are a connecting link between God and the situation or person you are with in any given moment. When you find God in yourself, your relationship, or in the situation, you experience true abundance. All is well. All things are working together for good.

A W A R E – A P Y

1. The next time someone judges or criticizes you, say to the person, "Tell me more." Once he or she has elaborated on the issue, again say, "Tell me more." If there is no more to be said, ask the person, "What do you need?" or "What's missing for you?" Be totally present to the person in order to discover his or her need.

2. Make a list of judgments that you have about someone. Your judgments are about what's missing for you. Identify what is missing for you or what you need that your judgment is really about.

3. Imagine that no one had the ability to judge another. Instead, people would simply ask for what they need or for what's missing for them. How would your life and relationships be different if this were your lifestyle and practice?

4. The Chinese verb meaning "to listen" has three characters that represent the principle of what it means to listen. Each character is made up of an image, and the images are heart and ear, paying attention, and two streams coming together. These images depict empathy (heart and ear) and becoming fully present to the other person (paying attention) for the purpose of creating something together (two streams coming

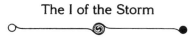

together). What if listening was not about hearing the words of another or understanding his or her position, but about creating something together? What insights do you have about the power of truly listening to someone? Can you see how this concept of listening might change how you manage disagreements?

5. How would your relationships be different if this became your listening practice?

6. Practice listening with these images in mind.

CHAPTER SEVEN

See It Right, Not Make It Right

Principle Addresses Misperception

THE SECOND ATTRIBUTE of wholeness is *Principle.* It is the *I* in the storm of misperception. Because everything you see or notice about yourself and your situation is viewed through the lens of self-worth, your seeing is incomplete. By definition, the perception of an adversary is evidence of misperception. Why? Because *no one* is against you!

Principle is another way of describing the nature of the universe, its order and intelligence. It is another word for God. Truth principles are ideas that organize our attention and awareness

upon the ever-present, unchanging order which
manifests itself as God's plan of good.

Truth principles can be divided into two
categories: faith-based Truth principles and love-
based Truth principles. Faith-based Truth principles organize your attention and awareness
on the presence of God in every situation. Love-
based Truth principles organize your attention
and awareness on your oneness with God and
all life. Truth principles don't change over time
and are the same regardless of culture or place;
they are the universal principles that remain true
for the human race, even as knowledge grows—
or ebbs.

Misperception occurs when *seeing is believing,* which is what we call judgment, or when
believing is seeing, which is what we call blind
faith. All human perception is incomplete and
is therefore misperception at the moment we
say, "This is it!"

Quantum physicists assert that in any given
moment, infinite possibilities are present. Some
go as far as to say that there are infinite universes coexisting. The moment you act as if
something is so, the universe of infinite possibilities collapses into one inevitable happen-
stance. When you look at something and say,
"This is what *it* is," you are pouring your creative energy (attention and awareness) into that
specific perception. The moment your aware-

ness locks on to one possibility, all other universes collapse. While in any given situation there may be many possibilities, innumerable paths, the instant you decree "This is it!" all others vanish. This is why it is so important not to give power to your perceptions, as if they accurately describe what is going on. When you realize that your perception is incomplete and mediated by your need to feel safe and okay, you will pause before drawing concrete conclusions. You must use Principle to compensate for misperception. Principle helps you manage the perceptual impairments associated with your conditioned awareness.

When you cannot see God at your point of experience, you may become fearful. When you don't feel connected to others, you may become suspicious. Faith is the avenue of awareness that sees God in every situation. Love is the avenue of awareness that sees your oneness and connection to all life. Gaps in your awareness of God's presence and in your oneness with others are what support fear and distrust. You move to the *I* of the storm of misperception as you work to fill in these gaps in your awareness. The key is to fill in the gaps with Truth principles.

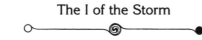

What You See Is What You Get

When we don't have all of the answers or all of the facts, we fill in the missing pieces in our awareness with beliefs about the person or situation. What happens when you apply misperception to any creative endeavor? What if what you make of something is not in keeping with the Truth of God? What you see is what you get! You must continually monitor how you are framing your experience. Ask yourself, "Is what I am seeing based on Principle?" You must see the situation right before acting to make it right. Principle frees you from creating out of misperception. Would you ever find satisfaction in playing cards with an incomplete deck? Of course not. It would be foolish, because you know that it would be a waste of time. So why then do you get so enamored by what you see, when all perception is misperception?

Principle Helps You See Through Misperception

Principle is the basis of seeing life as it really is, as God sees. In Unity and New Thought, we say that God is Principle. It is the high watch—the viewpoint of omniscience. Principle is the way of God-life. Principle is the order of the universe, the way things are in God. Principle is

the Truth, the Truth that stands the test of time—
like the Truth that no one is against you.

Principle helps you see through the illusion
of separation into the presence of God. Jesus
said, "For judgment I am come into this world,
that they which see not might see; and that they
which see might be made blind" (Jn. 9:39 KJV).
In other words, Jesus came so that those who
live from blind faith might see and those who
live by judgment will not. Jesus is the voice of
Principle in a world of illusion and separation.

Principle is the foundation of authentic action, or doing the right thing. Think of Principle
as the carpenter's level and square. Can you
imagine a carpenter building a house without a
level and square? Of course not! The level and
square are used as references to gravity so the
house can be built on a solid foundation. Truth
principles are also tools that help you build the
meanings and interpretations you attribute to
any given circumstance upon a solid, Principle-
based foundation.

Here's how Principle works like a carpenter's level and square. Take out your wallet or
billfold. Count how much money you have. Let's
say that you have seventy-two dollars. Based
on the amount of money you have, how pros-
perous do you feel? Now think of your bills or
your grocery list. Consider all the ways this
money will be spent. What makes this seventy-

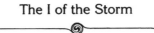

two dollars either not enough or plenty? Imagine you're in church and the offering basket is being passed to you. How much of this seventy-two dollars will you give? Will your gift be given from lack or will it be given from abundance?

How you see things is supported by a belief. In this case, a sense of lack or not enough is supported by a belief in lack. Now, is your belief in lack on the level? Is lack based on Principle? No, of course not. In Principle, there is only abundance.

Abundance is another word for *infinite possibilities*. In both the spiritual and the material realms, there is an infinite potential ready to meet your every need. This potential seeks to express itself through us as abundance. As we recognize this, we tap into the possibilities of the moment because our attention and awareness are based upon the unlimited universe. Your experience of lack only exists in context with the meaning *you* attribute to the amount of money you have.

Principle Helps Free You From Defensiveness

Let's look at another example. Someone judges you and you become defensive and uneasy. Whatever was said makes you feel small or not okay. You push back by justifying your-

self. You find yourself at the edge of your resourcefulness. You say to yourself, "See, what this person said *is* proof she doesn't like me." The interpretation may or may not accurately describe the situation. But the plot thickens as misperception deepens.

The key is to see the opportunity to shift out of your interpretation (which supports the defensive behavior) and into exploring the possibilities that underlie the experience itself. In other words, if the difficult situation brings you to the edge of your resourcefulness, isn't it true that it is only difficult because you lack the resource to manage it differently—with ease instead of dis-ease, with confidence instead of insecurity? After all, if you felt okay about yourself in the relationship, if your sense of well-being were intact, another's judgment might not be as hurtful, allowing you to experience the judgment as valuable feedback regarding the relationship.

The options available are these: You could reinforce the *meaning* that supports your interpretation and defensiveness. You could intensify your efforts to gather evidence that "this is the way it must be, because look at it!" Or you could become interested in discovering the missing resource you need in order to manage the situation without trying to make it (the situation) wrong or go away.

To discover what resource you are missing, simply ask yourself, "What do I need that I don't have (or didn't have) which would permit me to be present to the judgment, without needing to be right or make the other person wrong?" If your answer relates to something in the situation—say the need to have the person stop judging you before you can feel safe—you are looking in the wrong direction. What *inner* quality or resource are you missing? As you look inside yourself, you will see that you are missing a clear connection to your own sense of worth. If you felt whole and confident, you could see that the judgment is about what the *other person needs* or that it is about *what the relationship needs* or that it is about *what you said or did* which created some tension.

Shifting your attention from the feeling of defensiveness to the question What am I making this mean? allows you to reframe the experience as an opportunity to discover what's missing in the relationship. In Principle, no one is against you; therefore, *what you are making the experience mean* is the true enemy. The judgment is what got your attention. But it is Principle that helps you redirect your attention and awareness to the underlying needs of the relationship. Your former adversary reveals where you are lacking a clear, conscious connection to your own sense of worth. You see this by

looking at how you are inclined to react. But by not reacting to the judgment to make the other person wrong, you have the opportunity to create greater cohesiveness or intimacy when your focus shifts from self-protection to mutuality and shared purpose.

The Power of Perception

Jesus said to Peter, the disciple who represents faith, "Whatever you bind on earth shall be bound in heaven, and whatever you loose on earth shall be loosed in heaven" (Mt. 16:19 RSV). Another way of saying the same thing is this: "According to your faith be it done unto you." How you see things, what you make your experiences mean, and what you do because of what the experiences mean to you are powerful forces in your life. When seeing is believing or when believing is seeing, you are framing your life in no uncertain terms. Your perception is your reality. What you see is what you get. Charles Fillmore, cofounder of Unity, said that faith is "the perceiving power of the mind linked with the power to shape substance."[5]

Can you see how important it is to bring your perceptions into the light of Principle? And

---

[5] Charles Fillmore, *The Revealing Word* (Unity Village, Missouri: Unity Books, 1990), p. 67.

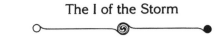

can you see that with an awareness of Principle, there is a different way of managing or relating to a situation which appears to be adversarial or against you? This doesn't mean that you must discount your experience or intuition. It means that you must include Truth principles in your interpretations of challenging situations and that you must respond to the situations from an awareness of Truth.

A W A R E - A P Y

1. Make a list of Truth principles. They are your keys to the kingdom.
2. Make a list of meanings or interpretations you commonly make about yourself or your life that bring you discomfort.
3. Next, draw a picture of a tree. Label each branch with one of the meanings from your list. Now consider how the tree has been planted in your life. Draw the root system. What false belief does each root represent? Label each root with a false belief.
4. Draw some fruit on the branches. Considering the root system and the branches, what does the fruit represent?
5. What do you notice about the relationship between how your life looks and feels and the underlying beliefs you have about yourself and life?

CHAPTER EIGHT

Living on Purpose

Purpose Is; You Are

THE THIRD ATTRIBUTE OF wholeness is *Purpose*. Purpose is the *I* of the storm of competing values, goals, and needs. Purpose is the universe's intention to be, through you, the presence of God. You exist because Purpose is. What is the universe's intention that seeks to live through you? In Unity, we call Purpose the *Christ of God,* meaning the whole and complete expression of God. Your spiritual purpose is to be the Christ of God, the Christ of your world. Jesus was the Christ of *his* world. You are the Christ of *your* world. Any lesser Purpose is sure to create conflict in your life.

The entire universe supports you in being the Christ of God in your world. Every challenge, every difficulty, every temptation is an opportunity to shift your attention and awareness to the question What is my purpose in this situation? Every challenge, every difficulty, and every temptation asks you the question, "Who are you, really?"

Jesus asked the disciples, "Who do people say that I am?" Peter, representing faith, said to Jesus, "You are the Christ, son of the living God." To that response, Jesus said to Peter, "On this rock [on the perception that the I AM is the Christ of God] I will build my church, and the gates of Hades will not prevail against it" (Mt. 16:18 NRSV). Life asks you the same question every moment that your life is on the line, "Who are you, really?" Go ahead. Say it: "I AM THE CHRIST, CHILD OF THE LIVING GOD." Say it again: "I am the Christ, child of the living God." That wasn't so bad, was it? The roof didn't cave in. Lightning didn't strike you dead.

You see, until you take complete ownership of your Purpose, to be the Christ of God, the Christ of your world, you will not find inner peace or wholeness. Now, I know what you must be thinking. You don't feel worthy enough to consider yourself on the same level as Jesus. Well, don't fret. You're probably not on the same

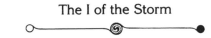

level as Jesus, but you are on the same journey. You are in the process of awakening to *God's* idea of you. Jesus is your role model, your elder brother. He demonstrated that with God all things are possible and he told us that we would do the same. It may take some getting used to. But eventually you will see that everything in you longs to be about this Purpose. Jesus called it his "Father's business." You wouldn't be reading this if you weren't already far into your spiritual journey. So proclaim to yourself: "I am the Christ of God, the Christ of my world."

The Way, Truth, and Life of God

This is your spiritual job description, your purpose for living. And believe it or not, everyone has this same purpose. This is why no one is against you. Even when it looks as if someone is your adversary or enemy, that person really isn't. This may not make much sense now, but as you practice living on Purpose, you will see that even someone's ill will has a way of transforming into a blessing. Remember, all things work together for good.

You are the way, the Truth, and the life of God. This is what it means to be the Christ. This is what it means to live from your wholeness. You may think that in order for you to be whole or feel good about yourself, you need to recover

from an illness or an addiction, get over a failed relationship, lose thirty pounds, quit smoking, finish therapy, or be forgiven by your children. None of that has to do with your wholeness and worth. Thank God! Your wholeness and worth are grounded solely in the expression of God's presence through you. And how that looks in any given moment is best described as being the way, the Truth, and the life of God.

The Way of God

Say to yourself, "I am the way of God." You *are* the way of God. You are either the way of God or you are *in the way* of God. Your entire being is created to be an expression of God. Everything real in you gives expression to God. Sometimes, however, you are in the way of God's expressing through you. It's important for you to know the difference—between when you are being the way of God and when you are in the way of God. Here's a hint: If you are judging, blaming, fearful, dishonest, unwilling, unforgiving, doubting, stubborn, unkind, or just plain negative, you are likely in the way of God. And that could be hazardous to your health.

Imagine picking up a young child and holding her close in a loving embrace. Imagine the love that flows through you to the child. When you love the child, is it your love which you are

sending or is it God's love which is loving through you? It's God's love, isn't it? You are simply being the way of God's love. And from the little child's point of view, your being the way of God's love or Jesus' being the way of God's love are the same. Do you see that?

Whenever you are allowing God to move through you, you are the way of God. A child's need for love invites you to open your heart completely, unconditionally, so the fullness of God's love can be shared. And in your experience of being the way of God, is there any lack? Is there anything that can make the moment better? Herein is a demonstration of true abundance. When you are the way of God, you experience the abundant life that Jesus told us about.

Now here comes the hard part. Imagine someone who has hurt you or treated you unfairly. See this person in front of you as you did with the young child. What's the difference? Are you *the way* of God's love, or are you *in the way* of God's love, which is loving through you to this person in the form of forgiveness or understanding? The difficulty you may feel in loving this person unconditionally is in the way of God. Do you see this? No doubt you have every justification for your feelings and good reasons for not warming up to the person. But can you see that you are literally in the way of God when

you are not willing or able to love in the same way as you would if this person were the child you so eagerly embraced? Is this person any less deserving of God's love? Can you see that had this person been loved the way a child is unconditionally loved, this person might have had a different relationship with you, a difference that might have freed both of you from being hurt or disappointed?

Can you see that *you* are the Christ of God in this situation, with an opportunity to be the way of God's love? Can you see that this person in your mind's eye is before you now because you are the Christ of God and that this person has come to you for love, for God's love? Will you open your heart to this moment when, from your wholeness and worth, you transcend the circumstances of human failings, separations, fears, insecurities, or the need to be right and do what your soul longs to do through you? See yourself embrace this person. Hold this person close and let the love of God flow through you like a river of life, moving you both to a new understanding and a new depth of forgiveness. And take a breath.

You are the way of God when you love unconditionally and accept people as they are. This stance of being the way of God is the *I* in the storm of interpersonal difficulty. You move from the circumference to your center when

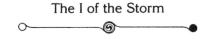

you ask the question "What does being the way
of God look like in this situation?"

The Truth of God

Another question you can ask is, "What is
the Truth about this situation?" No matter what
a situation looks like, no matter how terrible it
may seem or how awful it must be for those in-
volved, there is the Truth about it. It is your job
to be a witness to the Truth of God. The Truth
of God is the *I* of the storm of emotional upset
and confusion. You are the Truth of God. Say it
to yourself: "I am the Truth of God." What are
you doing when you are the Truth of God, and
how is it that when you are the Truth of God, it
is no different than if Jesus was being the Truth
of God in the same situation?

You are the Truth of God when you are a
witness to the activity or presence of God in the
situation. When you see God in the situation,
you are being the Truth of God. What is true in
all circumstances is God's presence. Your witness to this Truth is an essential ingredient in
the demonstration of absolute good. Your eyes
and mental faculties may not see beyond the
sights, sounds, and emotions of the moment,
but your awareness of Principle and your faith
enable you to hold the space of infinite possibilities open to the activity of Spirit. Your witnessing to God and giving voice to Principle

bring comfort and hope to those who are in bondage to appearances.

Jesus said, "You will know the truth, and the truth will make you free" (Jn. 8:32 RSV). This is how you know that you are being the Truth of God. Your witnessing frees you to see the situation as fluid, organic, and responsive to the power of prayer. Knowing the Truth frees the situation to become an ingredient in God's plan of good. Knowing the Truth frees those who are touched by the situation because an awareness of God's presence brings inner peace and awakening.

As the Christ of God, the Christ of your world, it is your Purpose to be a witness to the activity and presence of God. If you don't, who will? Think about all of the negative messages that envelop our lives like a noxious, invisible gas, choking us at every turn—friends, family members, and coworkers alike, all coughing up stories of doom and gloom such as troubles at the office, sickness at the doorstep, tragedy on the horizon. Imagine Jesus walking with his disciples as they came upon the impotent man who for thirty-eight years lay waiting for someone to carry him into the healing waters of Bethesda, and picture Jesus saying to him, "Gosh, I hope you get better!" Doesn't quite look right, does it?

Instead, Jesus said to the man, "Do you want to be made well?" Jesus was a witness to the Truth of God living in this man as the principle

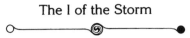

of wholeness. His question called the man out: "Rise, take up your bed and walk." Jesus' witnessing of the Truth freed the man to embrace his wholeness and worth.

That's your job too. Instead of commiserating with someone who is seeking sympathy, be a witness to the Truth. This doesn't mean that you should be inconsiderate of someone's feelings or be without compassion. It means, however, that you don't become embroiled in a story that says the *situation is who this person is*. You see this person as whole and worthy and responsive to the activity of Spirit at work in his or her life. If you don't, who will? Your witnessing to the Truth of God in his or her experience as well as your own is a true gift and blessing.

The Life of God

Another blessing to any challenge comes as you bring to the situation the life of God. You are the life of God. You are the "vitality, energy, vim of God," to quote a popular song, in those moments when the clouds of doubt, negativity, stubbornness, and futility threaten to storm upon the innocence of a new day.

What does it look like to be the life of God? And how are you just as essential to the situation as the life of God, as Jesus would be (if he were here)? When I ask this question at my

workshops, the audience becomes quiet. It's unusual to think of yourself as being the life of God, or alive in God. It's even more difficult to describe what that looks like. After a few moments of silence, I share with the audience the following poem from the *Tao Te Ching*, written by Lao-tzu, an older contemporary of Confucius, in about 500 B.C.E.

> Men are born soft and supple;
>   dead, they are stiff and hard.
> Plants are born tender and pliant;
>   dead, they are brittle and dry.
>
> Thus whoever is stiff and inflexible
>   is a disciple of death.
> Whoever is soft and yielding
>   is a disciple of life.[6]

You are the life of God when you create a childlike, youthful atmosphere around the issues at hand. When you are open, willing, flexible, affirming, and supportive, you are radiating the life of God in all that you are and do. If a conversation becomes blaming or condescending, you bounce into the discussion with openness and understanding. If people are stuck in

---

[6] Stephen Mitchell (translator), *Tao Te Ching* (New York: Harper-Perennial, 1991), p. 76.

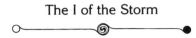

how a situation looks or feels, you remind them of the infinite possibilities that surround them. If someone gets upset, you help him or her look on the bright side and not take too seriously the opinions of those whose only purpose is to rain on the parade. You bring a playful energy to situations as you fill yourself with the awareness that you are the life of God.

Shifting Out of Competing Intentions

No matter what is going on in your experience and regardless of how you are caught up in relating to the issues at hand, you can free yourself of competing intentions the instant you remember your Purpose. If you are upset because your partner is not willing to follow your advice, ask yourself, "What is my real purpose in this situation?" Your real purpose is not about getting your way or about being right. The moment you shift into being the way, the Truth, and the life of God, something in the outer changes. You discover that no one is against you, that all things are working together for your highest good (even people who appear to be in your way).

If suddenly you find yourself in troubled circumstances, ask yourself, "What is my real purpose in this situation?" As you remember that you are the Christ of God, the Christ of your

world, you will quickly discover the divine appointment that awaits you. In some meaningful way, you have been brought to the kind of situation or person that needs your energy, your vision, your understanding of Principle, and your confidence in God. As you open yourself to the experience, you will see that with God all things are truly possible.

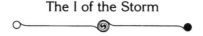

A W A R E – A P Y

1. Devise a plan to remind yourself of your Purpose throughout the day. Make sure it begins with the moment you awake and continues to the moment you end your day.
2. What do you notice about your day when you live your life on Purpose?
3. Recall the events of the past few days. Make a list of the situations and circumstances that challenged you. Can you see how it is possible that these experiences were a part of your Purpose, bringing you opportunities to be the way, the Truth, and the life of God?
4. Try to relive these moments from Purpose. How would you have related differently to these challenges? What do you notice about living on Purpose?
5. Make a list of experiences when you remember being the way of God. When you were being the way of God, how were you feeling about yourself and about life?
6. Looking at the challenges you have faced, can you see how you may have been in the way of God? Write a paragraph or two to explain.

CHAPTER NINE

Nonresistance Is Fertile!

The God Energy of Presence

THE FOURTH ATTRIBUTE OF wholeness is *Nonresistance*. You are the avenue through which the presence of God lives in this world. For this to occur, you must be present to life. You must show up. You must be present to win. Nonresistance is the *I* of the storm of defensiveness. It is the seat of wholeness and the contact point between heaven and earth—between the field of infinite possibilities and the needs of the particular situation.

Several years ago I presented a peace worker training intensive to a group of ministers and lay leaders near Savannah, Georgia. It was my

practice to begin our four-day schedule with an eight-hour presentation called "The I of the Storm." That portion of the training was the essence of what has become this book. Soon after things got started, we received word that hurricane Floyd was due to make landfall the next day. An evacuation order was issued, causing the cancellation of the rest of our training. Jokingly, the group blamed Floyd's presence on me. They tried to make the connection between my workshop title and the fact that the *eye of the storm* was on its way!

Affirming divine order, I proceeded to rebook my travel arrangements so I could depart with an appropriate margin of safety the following afternoon. My hosts graciously rushed me to the airport early the next day as they proceeded inland in compliance with the evacuation order. As I walked to the ticket counter, I noticed hundreds of anxious travelers in long lines waiting to check in. Then came the announcement which all frequent flyers like myself dread—an announcement which under normal circumstances would mean suffering inconveniences, delays, misconnections, and another bad meal in the airport restaurant. But this announcement was different. Instead of irritation, it struck terror: ALL FLIGHTS OUT OF SAVANNAH ARE CANCELED. PLEASE SEEK ALTERNATE TRANSPORTATION!

Suddenly throngs of people mobbed the

car rental counters, frantically seeking escape from the impending disaster. Because I could be counted among the frantic, I found myself noticing how silly I must seem to God. Here I had just spent a day teaching my colleagues the principles of being present to life, without conditions, without needing life to be different, and now I had failed to "walk my talk." Where was my Nonresistance? Where was my willingness to be at the *I* of the storm?

In that moment of awakening, I suddenly became calm and serene. I walked back upstairs and resolved to experience the eye of Floyd if that were God's plan for me. I focused my attention on my center and affirmed: *I am a calm, clear center of peace, radiating peace in every way.* Moments later an announcement came: "Passenger Simmons, please report to Gate 12 for immediate departure!" It turned out that I got the last seat on the only plane leaving for Atlanta.

Nonresistance and Communion are overlapping attributes in that being present to life without conditions means being connected to our experience—to whatever is happening in the moment without pushing it away, without any ifs, ands, or buts. While this is difficult to do in hurricanes and in the more mundane storms of our lives, it is the only way we can demonstrate the power and presence of God in the very situations we fear most.

Being present to life also means being con-

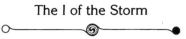

nected to your feelings and intuition. Being present to life means taking life into your center. When you are centered, you are relaxed and interested in creating a safe place for everyone in the experience, not just yourself. Being present to life means letting your center, your spiritual nature, move you instead of letting your fears or insecurities do it. If I had acted out of my fears at the airport, I would have rented a car and spent the day in a 16-hour traffic jam on the way to Atlanta. A movement from center is always an authentic response to a situation. Authentic action means doing the right thing. My center, my connection to God, moved me to sit still and be calm.

Shortly after I received my private pilot's license, I became eager to impress members of my church with my newfound hobby. My wife at the time (a past-wife experience) was an attorney with a law practice throughout the state of Arkansas. She frequently requested that I fly her to Russellville, Arkansas, where she was opening a satellite office. On this particular occasion, a church member also needed a ride to Pine Bluff, 150 miles southeast of Russellville.

I reluctantly agreed to the cross-country trek, because on one hand I promised myself that I would not let anything get in the way of preparing for my workshop on prayer, but on

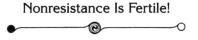

the other hand I wanted an excuse for not working on my workshop!

As usual, my wife was late getting started. By the time we got to the airport, we were in a rush. I hurried through the preflight sequence, checking the plane's exterior for problems, loose screws, air in its tires, and so on. As I opened the door to the four-seat Cessna, I noticed a note on the instrument panel: "NAVs and DG may not be working."

In simple English, the navigation aid and directional gauge were supposedly on the blink. I had had problems with rentals before, but nothing ever serious. (I once had my radio go out when I was trying to land. The tower had to give me clearance via a light signal.) I wondered if I should abort the trip, erring on the side of safety. It would take my wife two hours to drive to Russellville. She would be upset, as would the church member who had given up her seat in a carpool to Pine Bluff. I jumped into the cockpit and powered up the instrument panel. Everything looked good to me.

I decided that because it was such a beautiful and clear day, I could easily sail through the friendly skies by keeping a bird's-eye view of the roadways below. After all, I was not rated for instrument flying anyway.

We departed from Fayetteville's Drake Field

twenty minutes behind schedule but, with favor-
able winds, landed in Russellville an hour later.
Within minutes we were off again, heading for
Pine Bluff. About an hour into the flight, I became concerned because it seemed that I had
wandered off course. I radioed Little Rock air
traffic control for assistance. As it turned out, I
was forty miles west of my destination and
needed to double back to locate the airfield.
Apparently there *was* a problem with the DG.

By late afternoon we took off to head back
to Russellville. A strong westerly wind prevented
my passenger and me from enjoying the rest of
the ride. I became preoccupied with staying on
course. In an attempt to locate smoother air,
I increased my altitude. This meant that I could
no longer depend upon the ground for reference and course correction. I became anxious
about being way off course. I decided to head
for the Arkansas River and follow it east to
Russellville. It would take the guesswork out of
my navigation. It seemed as if the navigational
instruments weren't working either. Forty-five
minutes later we made a bouncy landing to pick
up my wife.

In all of the confusion and in the presence
of all the tension, I forgot to check the fuel level
in the wing tanks before taking off for Fayetteville. With only an hour of daylight left, I hurried
to get us back into the air. Heading west with

the sun in my eyes and a thick haze blanketing the horizon, I lost sight of the ground. There was not a cloud in the sky above us, but there was no telling where the Ozark Mountains below us were either.

All of a sudden, I realized that I couldn't be sure where I was flying. Without a clear sense of the horizon or the ground, an unskilled pilot like myself is easily disoriented. With the sun blazing in my eyes, it was nearly impossible to see the compass. With no compass, with no directional and navigational instruments, with inadequate fuel, and with mountains below, I realized that there were only three possibilities to consider: (1) the fuel gauge was broken and there was, in fact, plenty of fuel; (2) the fuel gauge was working (but they always put a few extra gallons in the tanks, don't they?); and (3) we were going to crash into the mountains and die or become crippled for life.

I hesitated in informing my passengers of the problem. How excruciating! I should have stayed home and worked on my prayer workshop! Then I did what most ministers would do when the worst is about to happen—I prayed. I centered myself in the realization that God was piloting the airplane. I stopped wishing that I were someplace else and began to listen for the guidance of Spirit. No sooner than I had resolved to make God my pilot, I heard a big splat on the

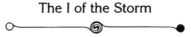

windshield of the cockpit. A large insect had managed to fly through the spinning propeller to make its transition squarely in the middle of my field of vision. Just great! I thought. You know how it is when you're driving through the country and a bug smacks in the middle of your line of sight? Well, here I was, contemplating my next incarnation, and this bug messes up my front-row crash seat. How poetic.

A moment later, I began to notice that if I lined up the sun with the bug's remains, I could fly in a straight line. Flying in a straight line is always better than flying in circles when you're running out of gas or are lost. The sun was rapidly sinking beneath the horizon when I took a chance to descend to an altitude just clear of the treetops and cell phone towers. To my amazement and gratitude, there was Drake Field and Fayetteville below. Thank God. Thank you, bug!

The next chapter explores the principle of Center and demonstrates the power of being centered as the foundation of Nonresistance and being present to life. There are four facets to being present. Think of an electrical circuit. To switch on a light, you must have a complete circuit between the power source and the light-bulb. The components of the circuit are the power source, the wiring, the switch, and the lightbulb. In the case of being present to life, you must be conscious of your purpose and

the intention of God living through you—this is being connected to Purpose, the power source. You must also be connected to your experience, like the wire is connected to the light. The switch in between is your willingness to be present to the situation. It is either on or off. Any resistance to the situation determines how much current will flow to the situation, just as resistance in an electrical circuit diminishes the brightness of the light.

As I mentioned earlier, according to Ohm's law of resistance, when resistance is reduced to zero, the entire potential of the power source is tapped. When you are nonresistant, you allow the infinite possibilities of God to flow through you to the situation. And conversely, when you place conditions or limitations on your willingness to embrace the moment, your resistance impedes the flow of Presence into the situation. Just as in the electrical circuit, resistance creates heat and deterioration of the conductor. When you get in God's way by resisting being present to your life and the circumstances that require the full expression of God to be on the scene, your resistance hurts you as much as it does the situation.

A W A R E – A P Y

1. Consider what it means to live life unconditionally. What beliefs or fears do you have that are obstacles to this?
2. Imagine that you are a dimmer switch. On a scale of 1 to 10, how bright is your light?
3. What areas of your life need more light?
4. What do you need in order to shine more brightly?

CHAPTER TEN

The Power of Center

The Power of Being Centered

THOMAS CRUM WRITES IN his book *Journey to Center:* "There is no true path without center./With center the mind, body, and spirit merge—/Passion and commitment unleash/A force that cannot be contained."[7] Central to his Aiki Approach® to conflict management is the principle of Centeredness. "Centeredness is a true psychophysiological phenomenon that affects everything in your environment."[8]

The key to embracing conflict is finding cen-

[7] Thomas F. Crum, *Journey to Center: Lessons in Unifying Body, Mind, and Spirit* (New York: Simon & Schuster Inc., 1997), p. 31.
[8] Crum, *Magic of Conflict,* p. 57.

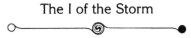

ter. You can't be nonresistant or present to your life experience unless you are centered. Being centered is a mind/body experience that occurs when your attention and awareness form a bridge between the experience and your center. Everyone has a center. It is a psychophysical place in the body. Your center is approximately 1½ inches below your navel, between your stomach and spine. In essence, it is your center of gravity.

Not only does every*one* have a center, every*thing* has a center too. A center is that point in space around which the activity of matter and energy are in perfect equilibrium. The eye of the hurricane is a center. The axle for a wheel is a center. The stationary point from which a pendulum swings is a center. Centers are both physical and intangible. There is nothing at the eye of the hurricane. Yet there is a functional place where the forces of the storm are in perfect harmony.

All centers have a single common property. They are never in conflict with any other center. Your center and my center can never oppose each other. This can be explained through the application of quantum theory. In quantum reality there is only one center. Every point in the universe can exhibit properties of the center. What this means is that your center and my center and the center of the universe are the same. I experience my center within me and

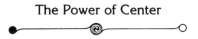

you experience yours within you. Yet your center is in the same place in the universe as mine. It's like the number seven. There is only one number seven in the entire universe. However, there are seven days in a week, seven brides for seven brothers, seven dwarfs, and even seven deadly sins! In fact, there are an infinite number of applications of the principle associated with this numerical idea.

So, a "center" is both a place and a potentiality out of which harmony and balance occur. There is a place within every relationship where the forces of personality and soul interact to create spiritual growth and transformation. On the surface, this place may look and feel stormy. But we have the capacity to experience the storm from *our center,* the *I* of the storm, where there is calm and peace, where there is an awareness of God's presence.

A Practice in Centering

Defensiveness is rooted in resistance. Resistance is triggered by a perceived threat. This should be a signal to you to shift your awareness to your center.

Stand with your feet and toes pointed straight ahead. Place your feet a shoulder's width apart. Relax your knees. You can let your knees slightly bend. Keep your weight centered between both feet. Place your left hand at your navel, and move your hand down three finger's length. Press your fingertips gently on this point. Place your right hand on top. Imagine a place inside your abdomen—a single point, like a spot! This is your center. See if you can bring all of your attention to this point. Now . . . breathe from center. You know intellectually that your diaphragm is doing the breathing but imagine that you are drawing in the air through a hole in your stomach just below your navel, a hole that leads to your center. Imagine and *feel* what it is like to experience the breath from center. It naturally allows the body to relax because the breath itself is arising from center.

For this next exercise, you'll need to get a partner. You be Partner A, and your friend, Partner B. Stand side by side, shoulder to shoulder, and facing the same direction. Partner B, using his or her arm closest to you, will place the palm of his or her hand, fingers pointing downward, at the center of your chest, just below your throat.

Partner A, stand with your feet shoulder-distance apart. Let Partner B slowly and gently increase pressure just enough to force you to wobble. What happens immediately? You push back, don't you? Your body instinctively resists the pressure because of the threat of falling backwards.

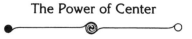

Now let's do this again. Without resisting this time, without pushing back, let yourself be tested again. With your instincts disconnected, it shouldn't take much pressure at all to get you to wobble. Most of us wobble at the slightest pressure! Partner B, make a mental note as to how much pressure it took to get Partner A to wobble.

Now reposition yourselves with Partner B's hand gently resting upon your chest. Partner B, don't push just yet. Partner A, become aware of your center. Bring your attention to your center. At the same time, bring the sensation of Partner B's hand to your center so that when he or she pushes again, it will be as if he or she is pushing against your center. Use your imagination.

Partner B, slowly begin to apply pressure to Partner A. Partner A, don't resist the pressure. Experience it from your center. Now, Partner B, take special care to note how much of an increase in pressure is necessary to move Partner A to a wobble or to a shift to resistance. It is likely that Partner A's centered state will require three, four, or perhaps ten times as much pressure to move him or her.

Moving Awareness to Center

Let's try to understand how moving your awareness to your center changes how you ex-

perience the pressure. As you discovered, you instantly shift into resistance when your body perceives a threat. Not to resist without an assurance of safety goes against everything that is in your body. The same is true when your emotional body perceives a threat. Your resistance is really how you try to protect yourself whenever you perceive a threat, whether the threat is real or imagined.

The other side of the coin is that just being pushed over doesn't feel right either. Being a doormat, allowing others to manipulate and use you, feels condescending and abusive. As you experienced, you wobble easily when you don't push back.

In the third part of the exercise, when you experienced the pressure from your center, you brought the experience into your center. You lived it from center. This is what nonresistance really is: taking life into your center. If resistance is pushing life away, nonresistance is taking life in.

While you became more stable when you became centered, the purpose of nonresistance and being centered is not about being more stable in your position. Even when you are centered, enough pressure will cause you either to resist or to take a step backward in order to remain connected to the pressure.

The purpose of nonresistance is not only to

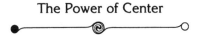

take life into your center, but also to know when to move and how to move appropriately. In the martial art of aikido, the practitioner moves from center to blend with the energies of the attacker. This appropriate movement and blending of energy allow the aikido player to value his or her relationship with the opponent, thereby ensuring that no harm comes to either party.

Think again of the exercise that you did with your partner. When you receive enough pressure, your center will move you. You will feel when you should take a step backward in order to stay connected to the pressure. When you're not centered, you move based upon your perceptions. If you see a tiger, you freeze, flee, or fight. When you get centered, you *embrace* the tiger because you experience it from your center, where you are in a natural flow of forces. If movement is required, your center will move you. If something needs to be said, it will be spoken from your center.

Extending Your Energy

Just by shifting your awareness from your circumference to your center, you change how you relate to the experience. You become present to your life experience and able to do the next thing, to extend energy.

The extension of energy is also a psycho-

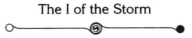

physical dynamic. When you feel love toward another person, your thoughts and feelings of love extend your energy field to your beloved. When you pray for another, your prayer consciousness is an extension of your energy to the other person.

When you are in conflict, you do the opposite of extending your energy. You contract. You distance yourself from your adversary. You avoid contact. While these tactics protect you from threat, they reinforce your sense of separation and exacerbate the issues that trigger upset. When you consciously choose to become centered, you naturally stay connected to your partner. This positive connection provides you with an opportunity to value the relationship by entering into dialogue and heartfelt communication.

Practice Makes Perfect

It takes practice not to become defensive or reactive when you are not accustomed to being centered. The metaphor of the *I of the Storm* is useful in remembering what to do when you find yourself caught off guard. First, shift your attention from the circumference to your center. Whatever has captured your attention, let it go. Don't make it an issue. Instead, bring your awareness to your center, to that part of

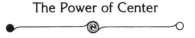

you which is rooted in wholeness. It's just as simple as the centering exercise. When you become aware of a threat or a conflict, just bring your attention to your center.

Your center has many handles. You can easily access it by asking yourself a question. Here are some sample questions that will get your attention moving in the right direction: What am I making this mean? How is it possible that this feels like a threat to me? What belief do I have about myself that supports this feeling I have regarding the person or situation? What inner resource am I missing in order not to feel uneasy in this situation? What part of me wants to push this away or make the other person wrong?

Once you have begun to explore the underlying beliefs that support how you are relating to the situation, begin to see that these beliefs are not you. They are simply the strategies you have used to protect or explain yourself. They are access points on your timeline, reminiscent of those early moments in your life when you didn't get what you needed from your caregivers. But now you have the opportunity to give yourself what you need in order to express your wholeness and worth, in a situation that mirrors one of those tender places in your psyche. Remember that whatever insecurities or fears you have, they are not who you really are. They were conditioned into you. You are bigger than your insecurities and fears because you are a whole and perfect child of God.

Ask yourself, "What do I need in order to be in this situation without needing it to be changed?" Give yourself what you need. Feel yourself connected to your wholeness and worth.

Next, bring the situation into your center. Live it from center. Ask yourself: "What does my center want to do in this situation? What does God want to do through me in this situation? What is my purpose, given that this is before me? What is authentic action, given who I really am? What is the right thing to do? What is the Truth about this situation?"

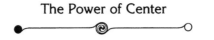

A W A R E – A P Y

1. What other methods do you know for becoming centered? Make a list.
2. Think of a challenge you are facing. What does it look like to move from the center called Principle in regard to the situation?
3. Think of the same situation in the context of Purpose. Give an example of moving from the center called Purpose.
4. The next time you need to face a stressful situation, practice becoming centered. What is your experience when you live the situation from center?

CHAPTER ELEVEN

A Call to Make Peace

FROM THE *I* OF THE STORM, you bring
the attributes of wholeness to the experience
of the storm. The purpose of your center is not
to make the storm go away. The purpose of
taking life into your center is to get what you
need in order to become fully present to the
storm. Being fully present in the midst of the
storm enables you to be the connecting link
between God and the circumstances that support the storm. As you relate from the intention
to create communion, you close the distance
between you and your partner. You bridge the
gap of separation and discover your oneness. As
you bring Principle into how you are relating
to the situation, you access the field of infinite
possibilities to create an explosion of opportu-

nity. From Purpose you become the avenue through which God blesses the situation.

Jesus said, "Blessed are the peacemakers: for they shall be called the children of God" (Mt. 5:9 KJV). I have always believed that peacemaking is a path to God. I have felt for myself and others a deep longing for reconciliation, not just in terms of healing in relationships or the resolution of conflicts, but in terms of my own sense of being. In a world that is so divided by issues of race, gender, sexual orientation, religion, and human rights, how is it possible that we do not feel both a part of the problem and a part of the solution? Reconciliation is somehow coming to terms with our fears and insecurities in the awareness that we are so much more. For me, peacemaking is a process of transcendence wherein we discover our innate wholeness and worth.

Peacemaking is neither passive nor aggressive. It is neither political correctness nor a militant demand. It is dynamic neutrality in the face of competing tensions or mutually exclusive positions. It is holding the space for the possibility of reconciliation to occur in a field of infinite possibilities. A peacemaker stands at the center of confusion, upset, and conflict without making others wrong for their positions. At the eye of the storm there is calm, clarity, and peace. At the *I* of the storm of conflict, there is

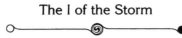

the oneness of Presence. A peacemaker invites disputants into the *I* of their storm so that from their center, from their purpose and their oneness of Presence, they can discover the missing pieces in their relationship. This discovery process is the first step toward reconciliation.

Day-by-Day Reconciliation

Several years ago, while closing a metal garage door, I accidentally pinched my fingers in the hinges. During the seconds that followed, amidst the excruciating pain, I experienced a total life recall. Similar in many respects to a near-death experience (NDE), my lucid consciousness became preoccupied with memories of moments and circumstances when I failed to live up to my own standards of integrity, when I had inadvertently caused harm or suffering to another. This was polarized by a sense of inner peace, calm, and feelings of euphoria. After extracting my ailing hand, I became aware of an urgency to make amends and reconcile myself with those whom I had mistreated or otherwise offended.

I made a list of individuals to contact or meet and promised myself that reconciliation would be my highest priority. Within a week, I contacted everyone. Much to my surprise, everyone on my list reported that he or she had no animosity toward me and felt that whatever griev-

ance or judgment he or she held was curiously dissolved days prior to my contact.

This unusual occurrence prompted me to investigate other NDEs to better understand and appreciate the significance of my own experience. I decided to conduct an experiment and personal study based upon my learnings. I posed the following question to myself: What would be the effect of intentionally, as a method of spiritual practice, simulating certain aspects of a near-death experience? Each night prior to going to sleep, I would practice a guided meditation ritual patterned after certain commonalities associated with NDE: having an awareness that death is imminent; being in the presence of a luminous being or divine entity; having a precise recall of past experiences with no judgment and having the awareness of the essential meaning of life; having a sense that if given the chance, I would awaken (return) with a transcendent purpose.

During the guided meditation, I imagined that it was my last night on Earth—that I would die in my sleep. As I engaged the prospects of death, I became aware of the events of my day (the recall was limited to events of the same day) and the ways my actions impacted people and situations. In the presence of Spirit, I asked that I be shown those instances where I failed to live from my highest and authentic Self, where

I had acted from selfishness, indifference, or insecurity and without love, understanding, or humility. I made a list of people or situations which surfaced in my awareness and promised that if given the gift of a new day, I would make it my purpose to first reconcile myself to these before any other personal agenda item. I called the process Day-by-Day Reconciliation.

Over a period of three weeks I endeavored to practice Day-by-Day Reconciliation as a means of spiritual development, creating a new list each night and fulfilling my promise to reconcile each item the very next day, whenever possible. As a result, I observed these things: (1) reconciliation became easier with practice, as did compiling each day's list; (2) those who I presumed were offended by me appreciated my contact, and as a result, those relationships became enhanced; (3) as the practice entered the second week, those on my list reported no memory of any offense taken to begin with; (4) as the practice entered the second week, I also awakened *instantly* when my attitude or demeanor fell short of my standards of integrity, thereby allowing me to relate differently to the individual in the moment, and consequently, my lists became shorter and shorter until the third week, when the evening's practice produced no lists; and (5) I discovered that my *reconciliation consciousness* manifested itself as greater harmony, well-being, and inner peace—both in myself

and in those with whom I had difficulty. I felt healed and transformed by the practice.

While the practice seemed to accentuate a state of mindfulness throughout the day and especially during my interactions with people, the remarkable by-product of the experience was seeing and experiencing a correlation between *intentions* in consciousness and manifestations of those intentions in my outer world. Just having the *thought* of doing the right thing seemed to manifest a correction in the outer. Whereas prior to a deepening of the practice, some outer action was required in order to demonstrate reconciliation consciousness, as practice deepened and intention became more authentic, the inner work produced an outer demonstration without an outer action being required.

Accept Your Call

You are called to be a peacemaker as a pathway to God and as a demonstration of your wholeness and worth. The entire universe supports you in making peace wherever you are and in every storm that comes upon you. No one is against you. Make your pathway to God a demonstration of this Truth, for blessed are you who have been called to make peace in a world that longs to know its wholeness and worth. Godspeed!

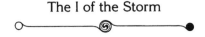

A W A R E – A P Y

1. Each day is a gift from God. Tomorrow is promised to no one. The fact that we awake to a new day is testimony to God's grace granting us the opportunity for healing and reconciliation. Imagine that tonight may be your last moments on Earth. In your sleep, the Holy Spirit appears to you and offers you a chance to leave this world free of any obligation or regret.

In an instant you review your life and each moment of fear, jealousy, greed, condemnation, dishonesty, prejudice, complacency, and arrogance you have ever felt. You see the consequences of not being connected to your wholeness and worth—the pain you have caused, the pain you have experienced. The Holy Spirit speaks to you: "Can you see that no one has ever been against you? Can you see that your fear and loneliness have been wrought in sheer ignorance of your true Self? Are you willing to forgive those who have harmed you in any way, realizing that you could only have been hurt because you were not connected to your wholeness and worth? And are you willing to ask for forgiveness and make amends from all you have placed in harm's way?

You answer, "Yes, yes, yes." The Holy Spirit then asks you to recall the events of yesterday. In an in-

stant you see the people and circumstances that you have impacted. You notice your own remorse and guilt over words spoken and unspoken. You see the unfinished business of your mission on Earth as the Christ of God. You long for the possibility to make things right, to be given a chance to take a higher path. The Holy Spirit tells you that if you are willing to become a peacemaker and make healing and reconciling tomorrow's purpose, you will be given one more day on Earth.

You awake in the early morning and make a list of the people you must contact or meet. You resolve to transform yesterday's indifference into today's glory to God. You arise and give thanks that your dream has been an invitation to live in the grace of God.

2. Tonight, before going to bed, review the events of the day. What unfinished business awaits you tomorrow? Were you too quick to judge or too busy to really be present enough? Make a list of people you need to talk to or letters you need to write. Make a promise to God that if given the gift of tomorrow, you will make peacemaking your life's work.

3. I invite you to commit to an individual Day-by-Day Reconciliation practice, as I have described, for a period of twenty-one days. Keep a journal throughout the practice. At the end of the practice, send me your stories and testimonies, and I will publish them in my next book. You may e-mail me at < unitypeaceworks@aol.com > .

About the Author

Rev. Dr. Gary Simmons is an ordained Unity minister. In his twenty-eight years of professional Unity ministry, he has pioneered three ministries as well as served on the Board of Trustees of the Association of Unity Churches. He is the Director of Integral Operations for the Association of Unity Churches International, responsible for the coordination and implementation of an integral approach to church growth and development. Previous to this role he served as Director of Peacemaking Services.

In 1993 Simmons began his innovative work in the field of conflict management. Combining his background of thirty years in martial arts with the metaphysical Christian principles of Unity, Simmons pioneered a

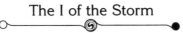

pilot project that introduced a new method of working with conflicted church communities. His success later led to the establishment of the Ministry for Peacemaking of the Association of Unity Churches, serving Unity, New Thought, and spiritual-based organizations throughout the world.

He also is author of *Embrace Tiger—Return to Mountain: Spiritual Conflict Management*, an audiocassette program, and a contributing author to *Sacred Secrets* published by Unity House. Rev. Dr. Simmons presents workshops and training intensives to Unity and New Thought audiences throughout the world. He resides with his wife Rev. Jane Simmons in Lee's Summit, Missouri, where he enjoys being a private pilot and an experimental aircraft builder. He received his doctor of theology degree from Holos Graduate University in 2007.

B0184